AUTUMN!

idea book

a creative idea book for the elementary teacher

written and illustrated
by
Karen Sevaly

poems by
Margaret Bolz

Printed in U.S.A.

ISBN-13 978-0-439-49960-6
ISBN-10 0-439-49960-7

Table of Contents

This book is dedicated to
teachers and children
everywhere!

Notes:

Let's
Make
It!
GLUE

Let's Make It!

Children are especially responsive to the various holidays and themes associated with the four seasons. With this in mind, Teacher's Friend has published the "Autumn" Idea Book to assist teachers in motivating students.

WHO USES THIS BOOK:

Preschool and elementary teachers along with scout leaders, Sunday school teachers and parents all love the monthly and seasonal idea books. Each idea or craft can easily be adapted to fit a wide range of abilities and grade levels. Kindergartners can color and cut out the simple, bold patterns while older students love expanding these same patterns to a more complex format. Most of the ideas and activities are open-ended. Teachers may add their own curriculum appropriate for the grade level they teach. Young children may practice number, color or letter recognition while older students may like to drill multiplication facts or match homophones.

WHAT YOU'LL FIND IN THIS BOOK:

Teachers and parents will find a variety of crafts, activities, bulletin board ideas and patterns that complement the monthly holidays and seasonal themes. Children will be delighted with the booklet cover, bingo cards, nametags, mobiles, place cards, writing pages and game boards. There is also a special section devoted to the sport of the season!

HOW TO USE THIS BOOK:

Every page of this book may be duplicated for individual classroom use. Some pages are meant to be used as duplicating masters or student worksheets. Most of the crafts and patterns may be copied onto construction paper or printed on index paper. Children can then make the crafts by coloring them using crayons or colored markers and cutting them out. Many of the pages can be enlarged with an overhead or opaque projector. The patterns can then be used for door displays, bulletin boards or murals.

Making mobiles is especially fun for all ages. Teachers may like to simplify mobile construction for young children by using one of these ideas.

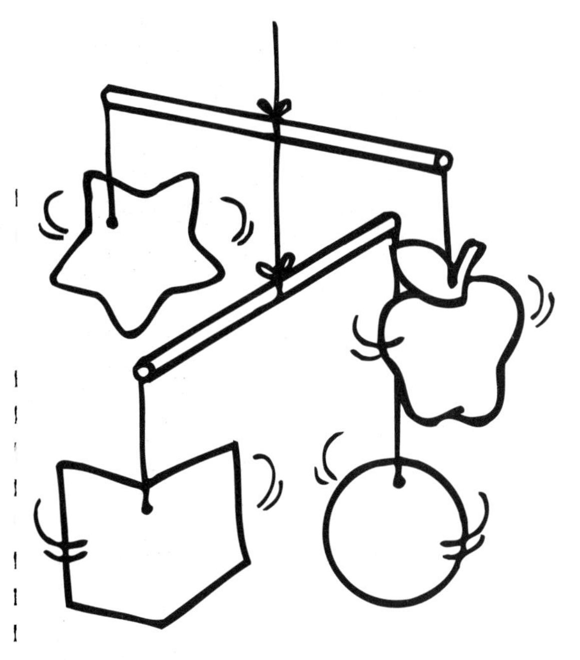

DRINKING STRAW MOBILE

Thread a piece of yarn through a plastic drinking straw and tie a mobile pattern to each end. Flatten a paper clip and bend it around the center of the straw for hanging. The mobile can easily be balanced by adjusting the yarn. (Older students can make their mobiles the same way but may wish to add additional levels by hanging other mobiles directly below the first.)

CLOTHES HANGER MOBILE

Mobiles can easily be made with a wire clothes hanger, as shown. Just tie each pattern piece to the hanger with thread, yarn or kite string.

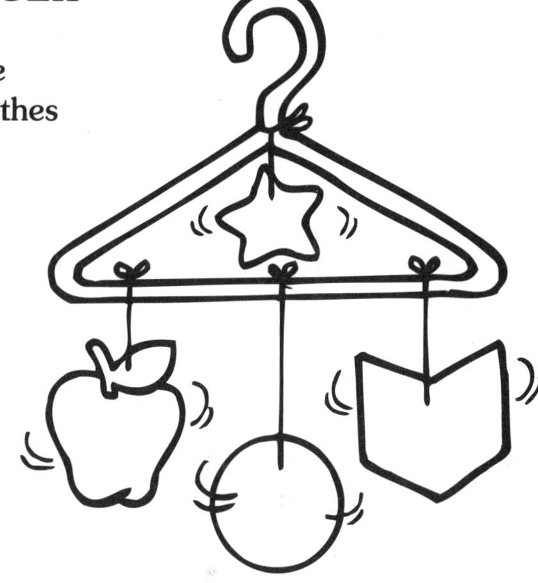

YARN MOBILE

Gluing the pattern pieces to a length of yarn makes the most simple mobile, each piece spaced directly beneath the other. Tie a bow at the top and hang in a window or from the ceiling.

CLIP ART PAGES:

The illustrations on these pages may be used in classroom bulletins, newsletters, notes home or just to decorate your own worksheets. Copy the clip art pages, cut out the illustrations you want, and paste them to your original before printing. The drawings may be enlarged or reduced on a copy machine. You are also free to enlarge the illustrations for other uses, such as bulletin boards, calendar decorations, booklet covers and awards.

PLACE CARDS OR NAMETAGS:

If possible, laminate the finished nametags or place cards after you have copied them onto colored index paper. Use a dry transfer marker or dark crayon to write each name on the laminated surface. After the special day, simply wipe off the names with a tissue for use at another time.

POETRY:

Children love simple, clever poetry. Use the poems in this book to inspire your students. You may want to have the students rewrite the poems for a timely record of their advancing handwriting skills.

Each morning, copy one or two lines, or an entire poem, on the class board. Ask the children to copy it in their best handwriting. Instruct them to write the date at the top of the page. Collect the poem pages and organize them chronologically in individual folders. This is a great way to show parents how their child's handwriting has improved throughout the year.

STAND-UP CHARACTERS:

All of the stand-up characters in this book can easily be made from construction or index paper. Children can add the color and cut them out. The characters can be used as table decorations, name cards or used in a puppet show. Several characters can also be joined at the hands, as shown. The characters can also be enlarged on poster board for a bulletin board display or reduced in size for use in a diorama or as finger puppets.

BULLETIN BOARDS:

Creating clever bulletin boards can be a fun experience for you and your students. Many of the bulletin board ideas in this book contain patterns that the students can make themselves. You simply need to cover the board with bright paper and display the appropriate heading. Students can make their own pumpkins for a classroom pumpkin patch or creative writing apples for a Johnny Appleseed display.

Many of the illustrations in this book can also be enlarged and displayed on a bulletin board. Use an overhead or opaque projector to do your enlargements. When you enlarge a character, think BIG! Figures three, four or even five feet tall can make a dramatic display. Use colored butcher paper for large displays eliminating the need to add color with markers or crayons.

WHATEVER YOU DO...

Have fun using the ideas in this book. Be creative! Develop your own ideas and adapt the patterns and crafts to fit your own curriculum. By using your imagination, you will be encouraging your students to be more creative. A creative classroom is a fun classroom! One that promotes an enthusiasm for learning!

AUTUMN ACTIVITIES
AUTUMN SEQUENCE CARDS
AUTUMN BULLETIN BOARDS
MR. SCARECROW
AUTUMN MOBILE
FLAPPING OWL CRAFT

AUTUMN TIME ACTIVITIES!

AUTUMN POEM

Carve a pumpkin for Halloween.
Two triangle eyes and a nose between,
A smile with three or four lifelike teeth,
Two above and a couple beneath.
The inside pulp bakes into pie;
Add cream and sugar, place oven on high.
Fallen leaves I will be raking
While the autumn pie is baking.
Winds blow kites in the harvest sky.
I can't wait to eat pumpkin pie.

COLLECTING LEAVES

Children love to collect autumn leaves. Many can be found on the ground but some may need to be picked. Ask students to be extra careful when picking living leaves so as not to damage the tree or branches.

Instruct them to find leaves with unusual colors and shapes. A display can be made in the classroom with signs noting the names of the trees. Students might also like to examine the leaves with a microscope or magnifying glass.

CHART A TREE

Select a deciduous tree on the school grounds. Have your students visit the tree in autumn, winter and spring noting the changes each season. Ask them to draw pictures of each change or take photographs and display them on the class bulletin board.

SEASONAL IMPROVISATION

Ask your students to act out the life of a leaf. The children will love pantomiming the growth of a new leaf, blowing in the wind, changing color and floating to the ground.

OH, GOLDEN LEAVES!

Oh, golden leaves, come tumbling down
To make a carpet for the town,
To fly above each busy street
And get beneath the people's feet,
To rustle as the cold winds blow
And make a welcome for the snow,
To leave the trees all brown and bare
And clothe the cold ground everywhere.
You looked so bright and green last spring,
A bright vibrant living thing.
You're wrinkled, crinkled, brown and gold,
You look as though you're mighty old.
You only last for weeks and days
Because spring weather never stays
But leaves us when you're turning gold,
Then autumn comes with wind so cold.
'Tis then you tumble all around
To make a carpet for the ground
To make a chilly atmosphere
And shout to all, "Winter is here!"

AUTUMN BINGO!

This game offers an exciting way to introduce students to the autumn season. Give each child a copy of the bingo words listed below or write the words on the chalkboard. Ask students to write any 24 words on his or her bingo card. Use the same directions you might use for regular bingo.

BACK TO SCHOOL BINGO WORDS

AUTUMN	PUMPKINS	TURKEY	GHOSTS
FALL	CORN	PILGRIMS	WITCH
SEASON	ACORNS	INDIANS	TRICK OR TREAT
HARVEST	APPLES	MAYFLOWER	COSTUME
BOUNTY	JOHNNY APPLESEED	COLUMBUS	JACK O' LANTERN
SEPTEMBER	SCARECROW	NINA	SKELETON
OCTOBER	THANKSGIVING	PINTA	BATS
NOVEMBER	FEAST	SANTA MARIA	BLACK CAT
LEAVES	CORNUCOPIA	VOYAGE	FOOTBALL
TREES	FAMILY	HALLOWEEN	ELECTION

AUTUMN
BINGO
FREE

AUTUMN NEWS!

A NOTE HOME TO PARENTS!

AUTUMN SEQUENCE CARDS!

AUTUMN BULLETIN BOARDS!

CAT-TALES!
Have students make their own "cattails" or "cat-tales" from the patterns on page 20. Students can write their own autumn poems or riddles inside. Display the "cat-tales" with lots of green paper leaves to create an effective autumn bulletin board.

"NUTS!"
Students will love displaying their own "nut" (or acorn) on the class bulletin board. Each child can add his or her own funny face and name to the acorn pattern. Hang the nuts from a paper branch or autumn tree displayed on the class board.

HARVEST THE FACTS!
Liven up a dull classroom with a ready-to-pick corn-field. Add your own math problems to the corn on the cob pattern and display several on the classroom board. Students can review their facts by opening each ear of corn and discovering the correct answer.

Corn on the Cob

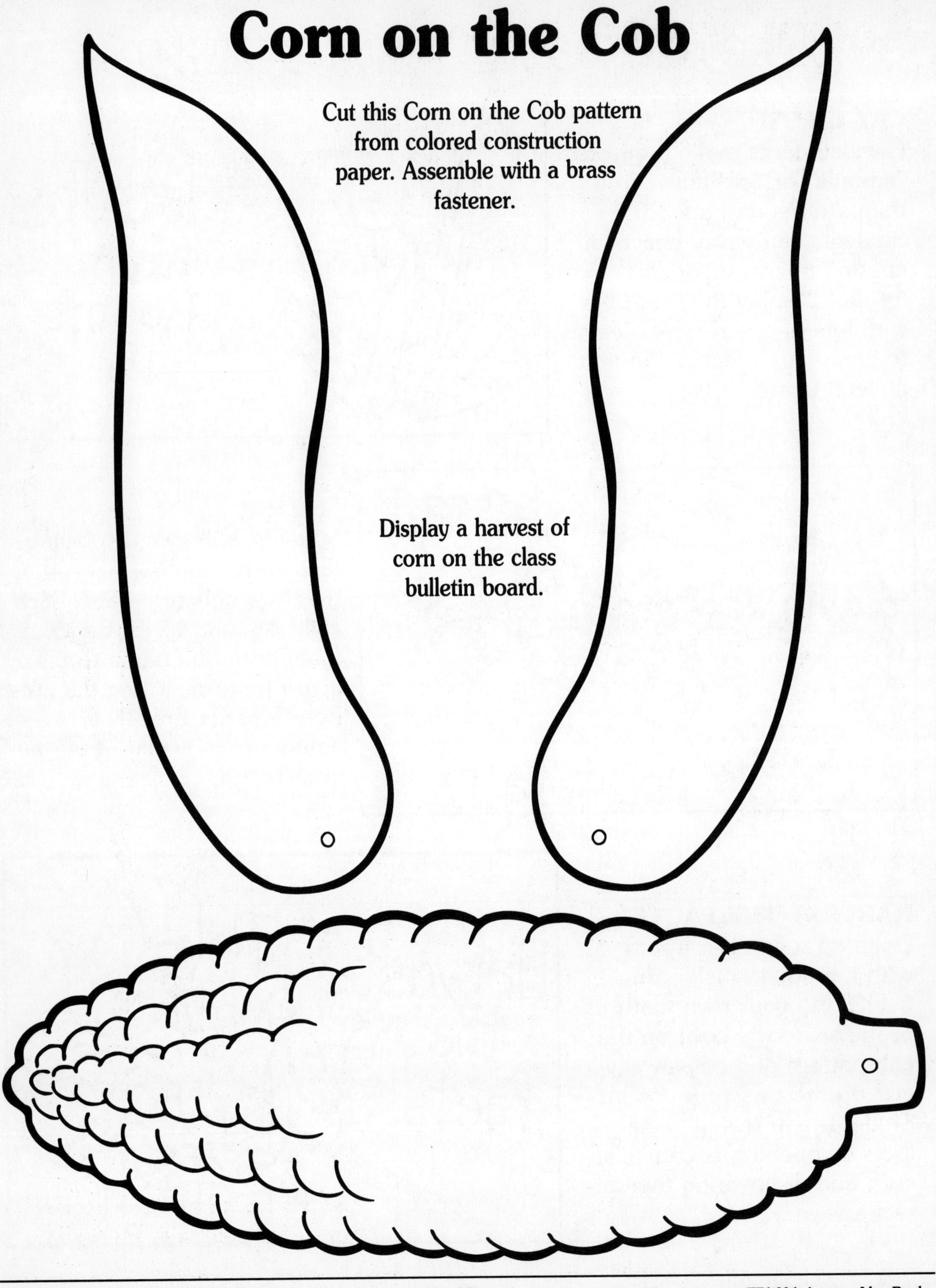

Acorn Pattern

Use this acorn pattern for booklet covers or a bulletin board display.

Cattails

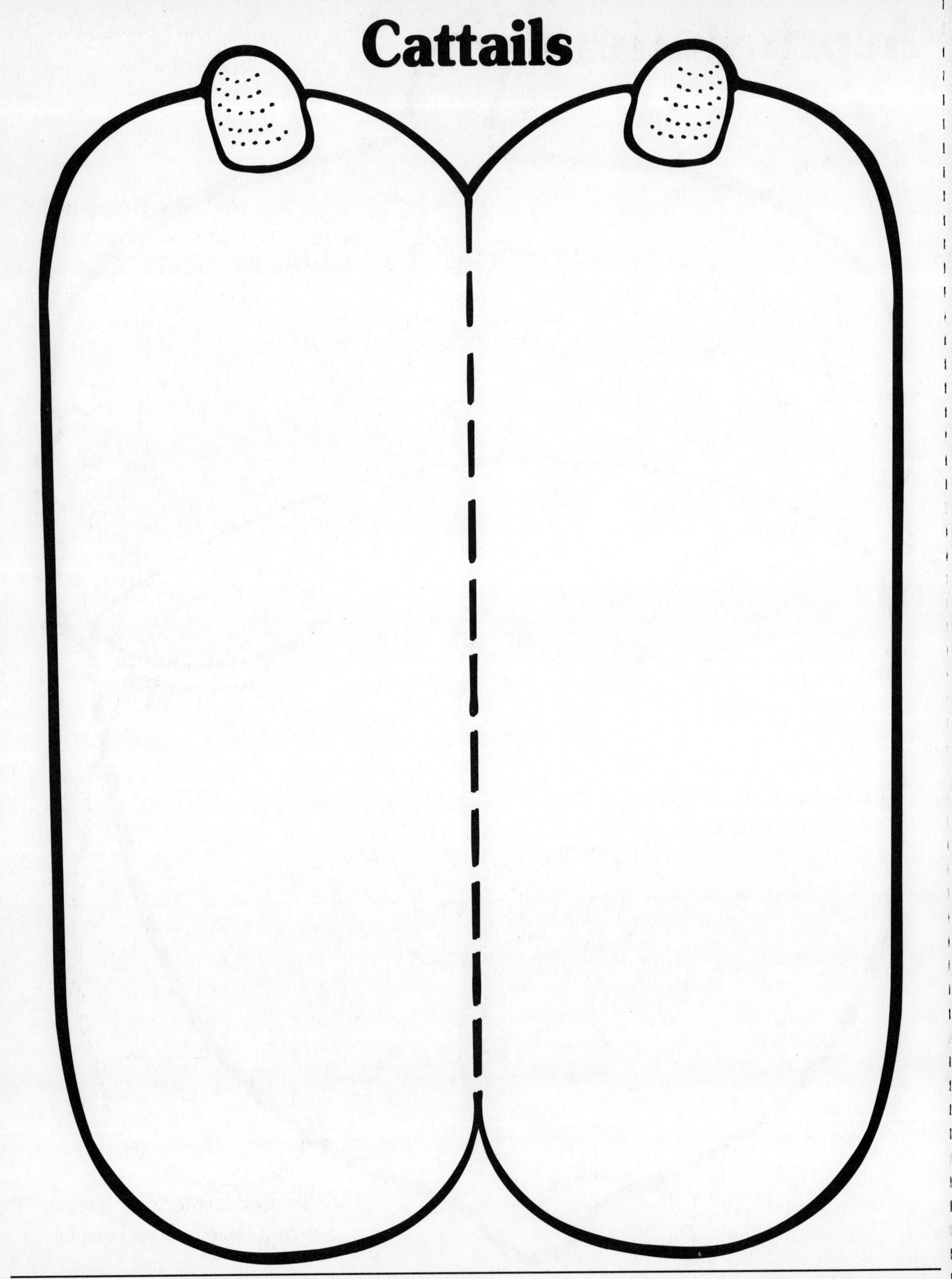

Mr. Scarecrow

Mr. Scarecrow can be enlarged for a class bulletin board or used in the size shown.

Cut the scarecrow patterns from colored construction paper. Color with crayons or colored markers. Assemble with brass fasteners.

Cut out the crow and place him on the scarecrow's shoulder.

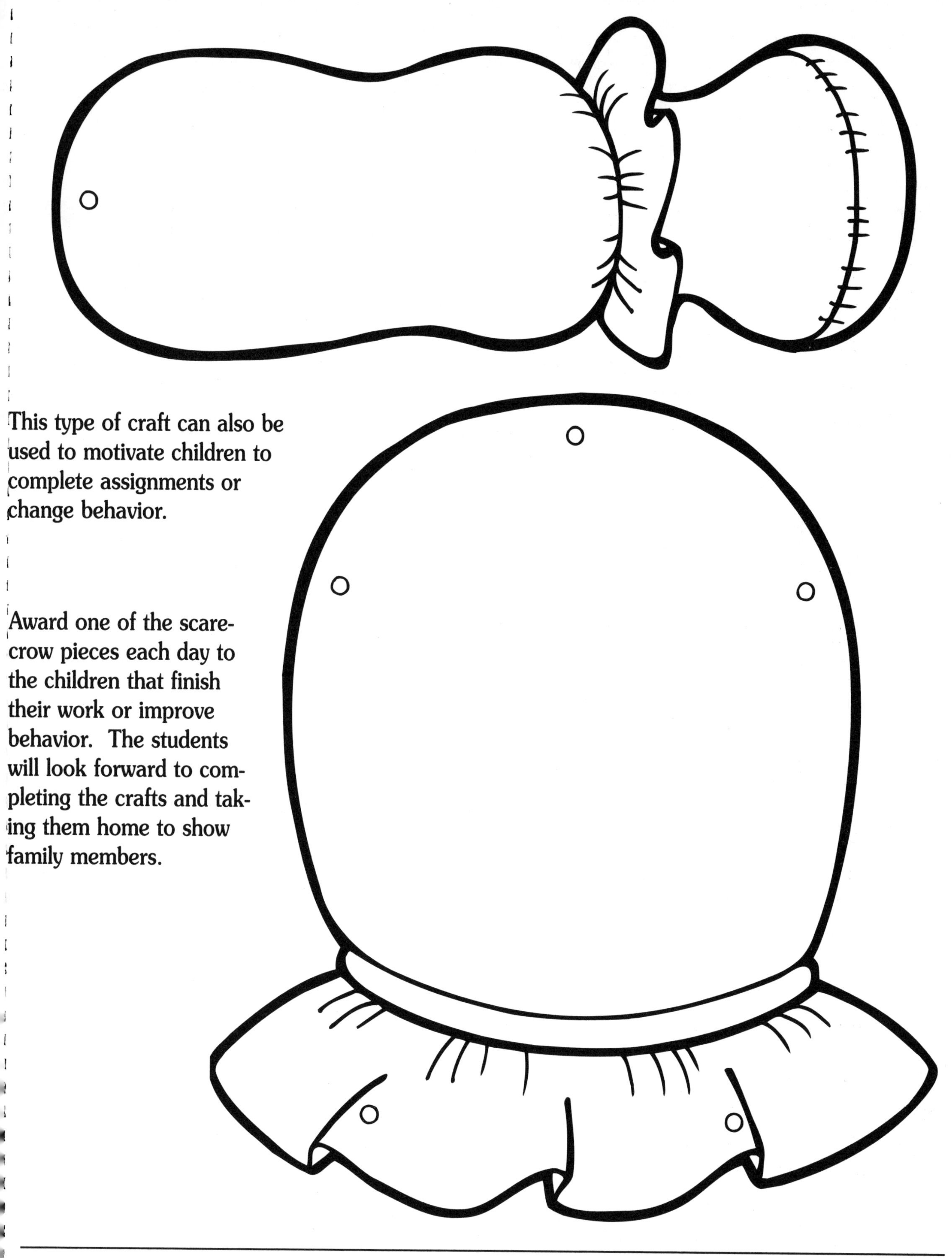

This type of craft can also be used to motivate children to complete assignments or change behavior.

Award one of the scare-crow pieces each day to the children that finish their work or improve behavior. The students will look forward to completing the crafts and taking them home to show family members.

Autumn Mobile

Each child can make his or her own Autumn Mobile by cutting these pattern pieces from colored construction paper. (They may want to mount the finished pieces on poster board for added durability.)

The autumn patterns can also be used as nametags or calendar decorations.

Children can list their favorite autumn activities on the hanging mobile pieces.

Flapping Owl

Cut this flapping owl pattern and his two wings from brown construction paper.

Assemble with two brass fasteners.

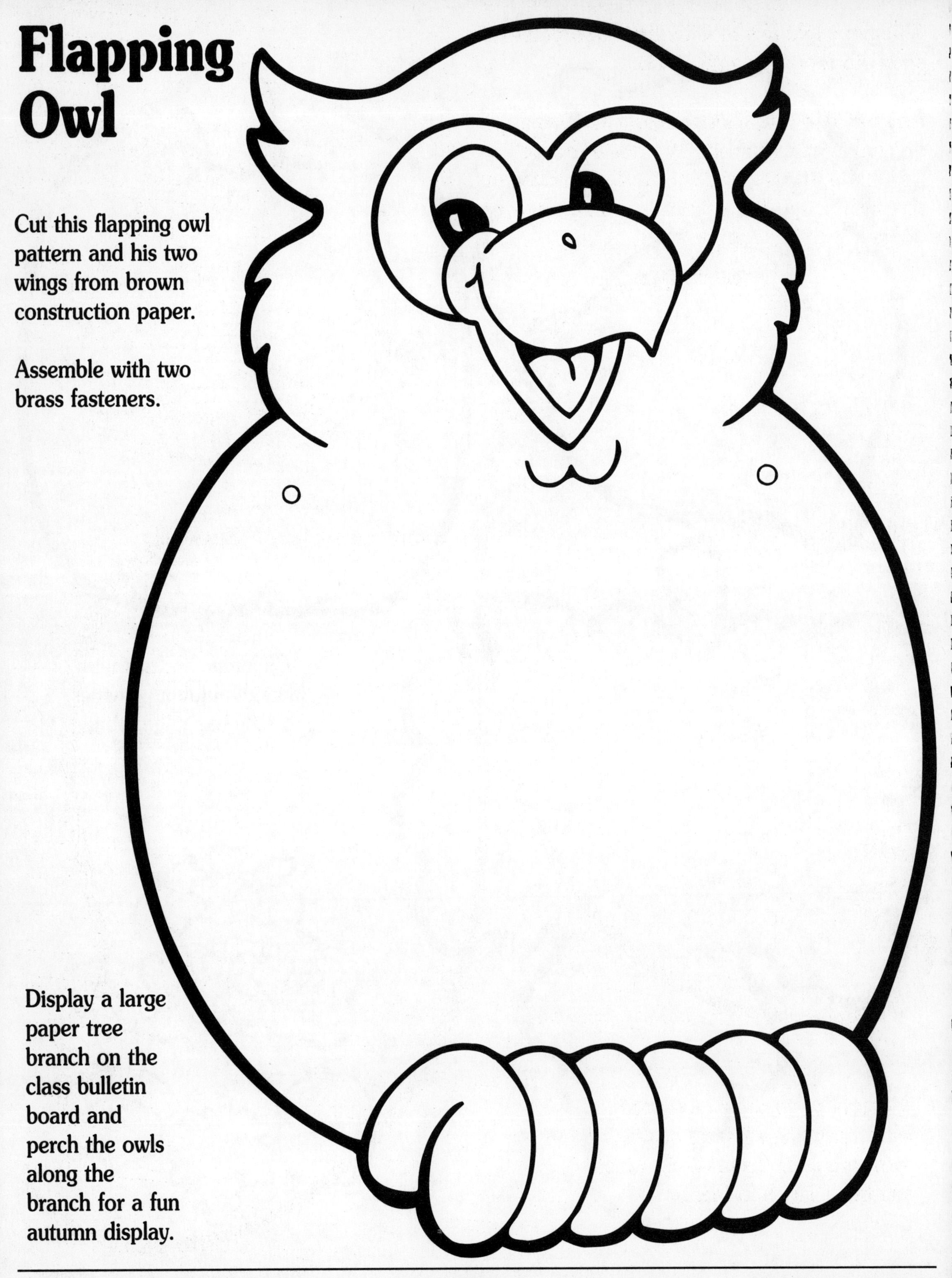

Display a large paper tree branch on the class bulletin board and perch the owls along the branch for a fun autumn display.

Children might like to write their own poems or short stories on the owl's body.

Another idea is to have the students create original autumn riddles. The riddle can be written on the wings and the answer written on the owl's body. The children can move his wings to find the answer.

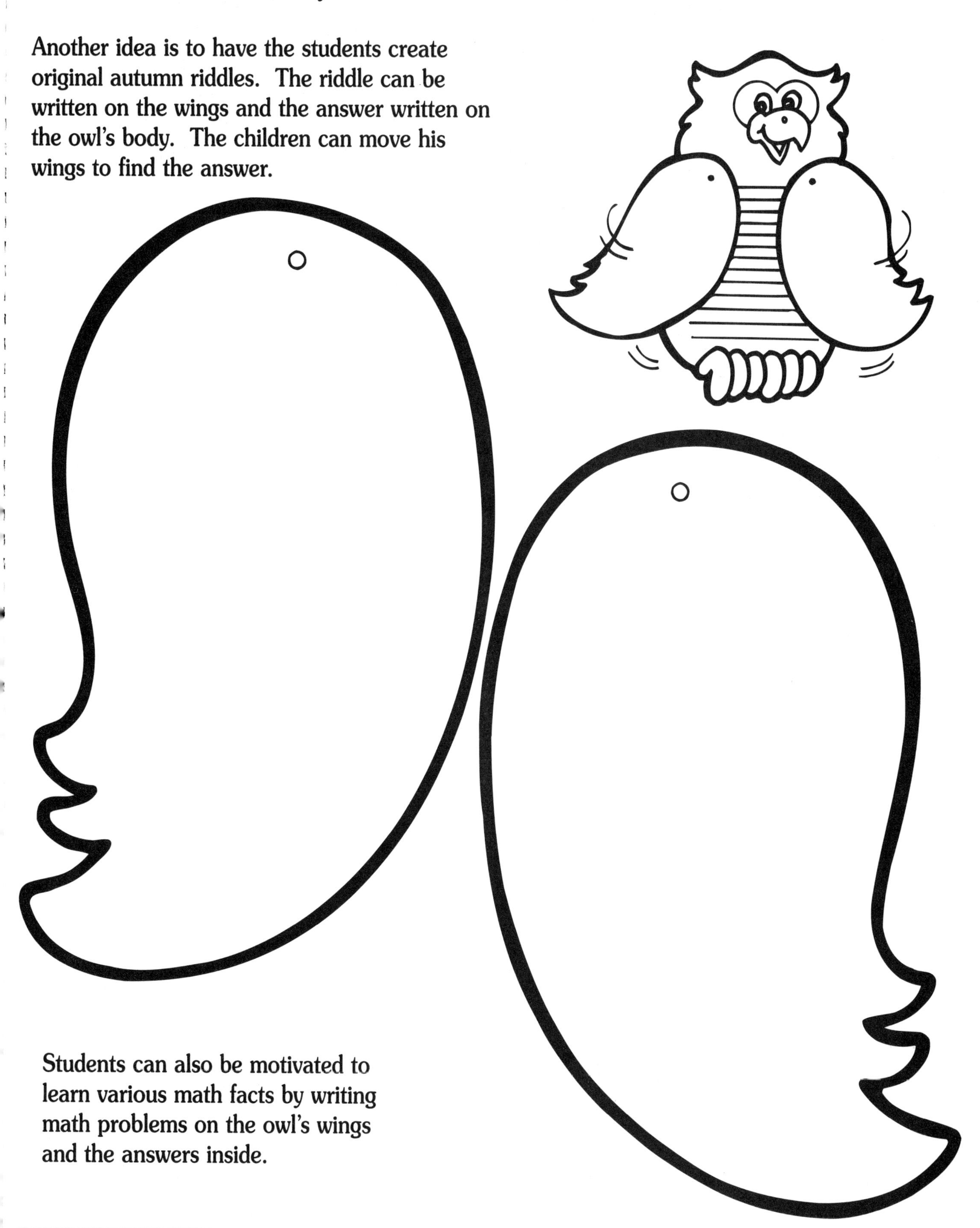

Students can also be motivated to learn various math facts by writing math problems on the owl's wings and the answers inside.

Creative Writing Leaf

Write a poem or short story about autumn.

SEPTEMBER CLIP ART
SEPTEMBER AWARDS
LABOR DAY
SEPTEMBER BULLETIN BOARDS
APPLE SEQUENCE CARDS
APPLE FUN GLASSES
APPLE TIME ACTIVITIES
JOHNNY APPLESEED CHARACTER
MATCHING APPLES AND WORMS
STAND-UP WORM
GRANDPARENT'S DAY
I'M SPECIAL MOBILE

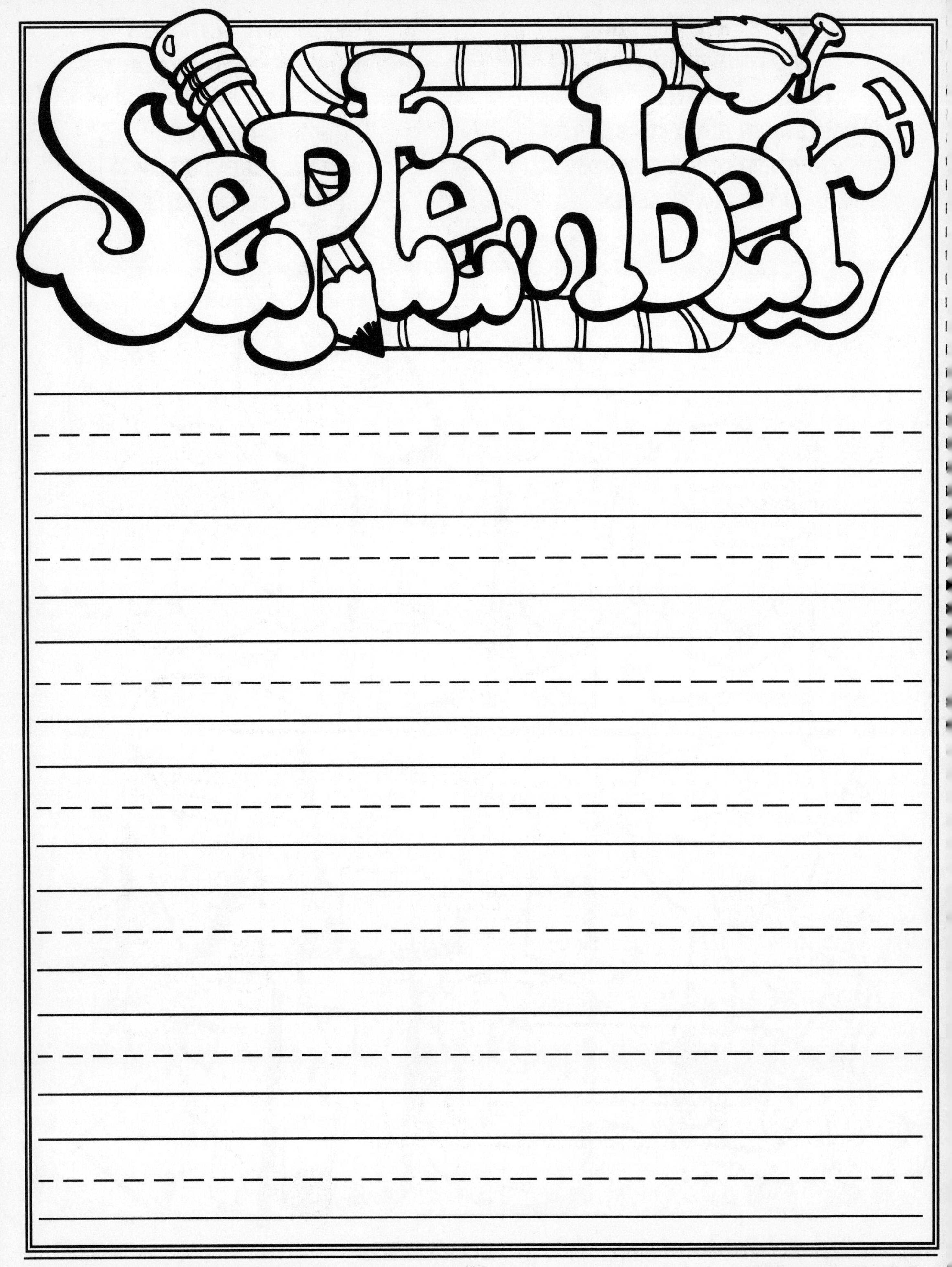
September

September Clip Art

SEPTEMBER NEWSLETTER!

TEACHER:	RM# DATE:

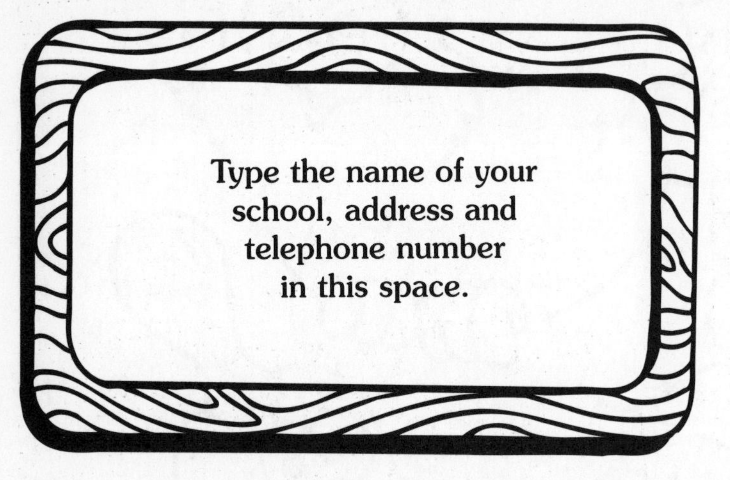

SUGGESTIONS FOR A SEPTEMBER NEWSLETTER:

- Welcome all of your students to the first day of school. Make sure that you inform parents of the time school starts and what their child should bring with them that first day.
- Tell the students and parents a little about yourself.
- Briefly describe your goals and expectations for the new school year.
- Remind parents to send their child to school with a good night's sleep and a nutritious breakfast.
- List your classroom rules and homework policy.
- Tell about your student of the week program.
- Staple a September cafeteria menu to each newsletter.
- Ask your school principal to write a brief message that can be included with the September newsletter.
- Note the date of Labor Day and make sure that parents know which days children will not be in attendance.

- Ask for parent volunteers and home room mothers and fathers.
- Tell about the special things your class will be working on in the next few weeks.
- Outline the schedule of a normal day's activities.

SUPER STUDENT AWARD!

awarded to

____

for

____

____

____

____

Date

____

Teacher

STUDENT OF THE MONTH

AWARDED TO

____

Name

____

______________________________ ______________________________

Teacher Date

LABOR DAY!

SEPTEMBER'S LABOR DAY

This month summer will conclude
Fall comes with colder attitude.
There's a special holiday, remember?
Very first Monday in September.
President Cleveland thought it best
For working people to have a rest,
That a holiday be known
As working people's very own.
Labor Day, a day of vacation,
For picnics, parades and recreation.

LABOR DAY

This special day, observed on the first Monday of September, is dedicated to the working people of America.

You might use this time to acquaint your students with the different workers at your school or in your neighborhood. You might like to ask the local dentist or auto mechanic to come and talk about their job with your students. Labor Day will give you an opportunity to introduce your students to many different jobs and careers available in your community. Here are a few suggestions:

1. Ask the school nurse to speak to your class about careers in the medical field. She might like to teach the students how to take their own temperature or pulse.

2. Plan a special "Career Day." Invite parents or local merchants to come to your class and talk about their occupations.

3. Children that are interested in agriculture might like to plant and care for a school garden. They could even sell fresh vegetables during lunchtime.

4. Create a simple job application that can be filled out by your students for classroom duties. They might apply for the position of chalkboard monitor or class librarian.

5. Encourage some of your students to start a classroom newspaper. Students can assume the duties of publisher, editor, reporter, proofreader, artist, photographer and printer.

SEPTEMBER BULLETIN BOARDS!

BRANCHING OUT!

Create a year-round bulletin board by arranging a paper tree branch on the class board. Children can cut autumn leaves that can be pinned to the branch. Label the leaves with book titles for a library display or students' names for a "Welcome Back to School!" greeting.

GOING, GOING GONE!

Display these colorful apples for a sequential autumn bulletin board. Emphasize the apple theme by making baked apples or applesauce with your students.

WE ALL FIT IN!

Cut enough puzzle pieces from one large sheet of paper so that each child has a piece. Label each puzzle piece with a child's name and have the students reassemble the puzzle on the class board.

This clever idea will help students know that they are an important part of the whole class.

APPLE SEQUENCE CARDS!

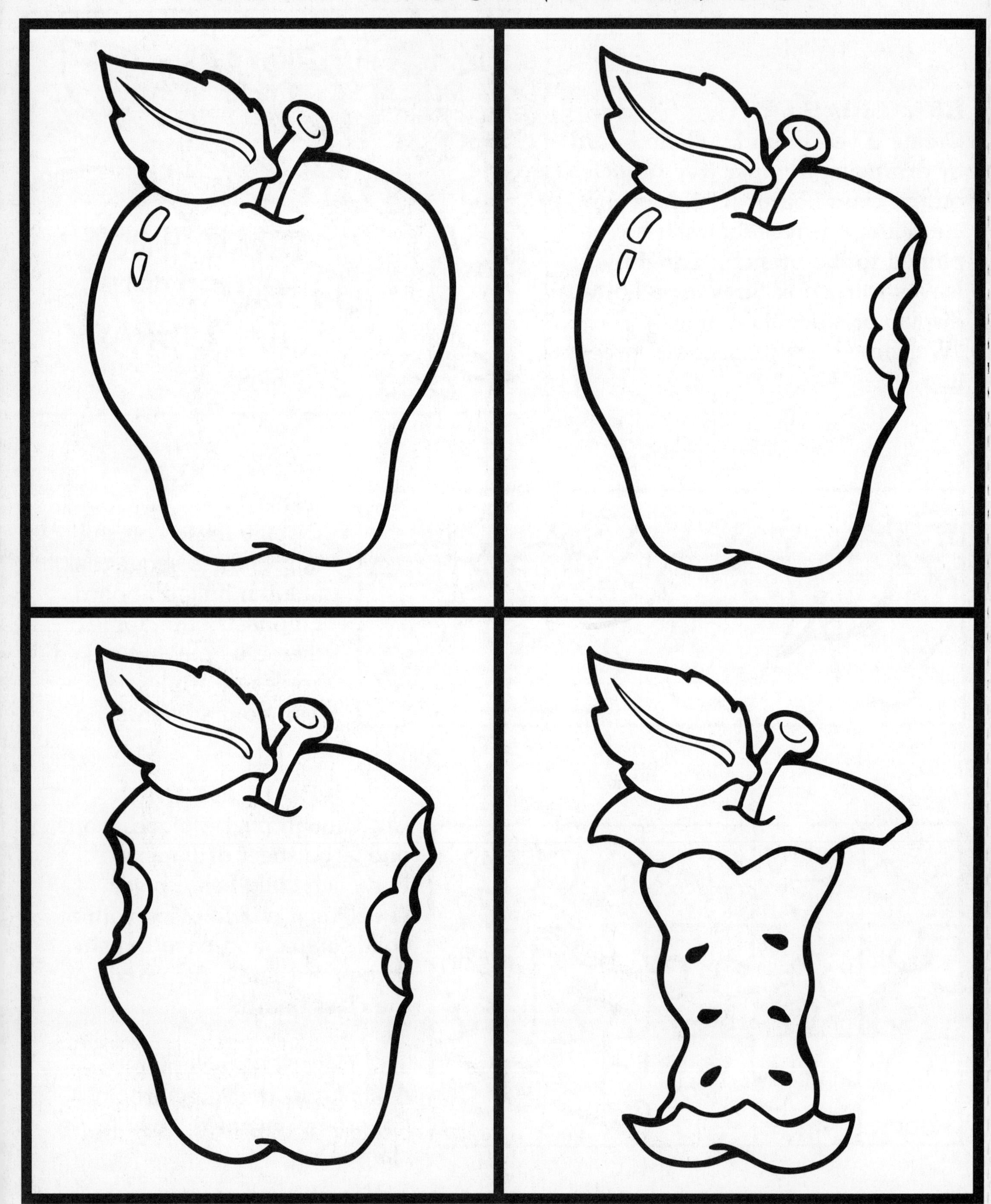

Apple Fun Glasses

Children will love making and wearing these "Apple Fun Glasses!"

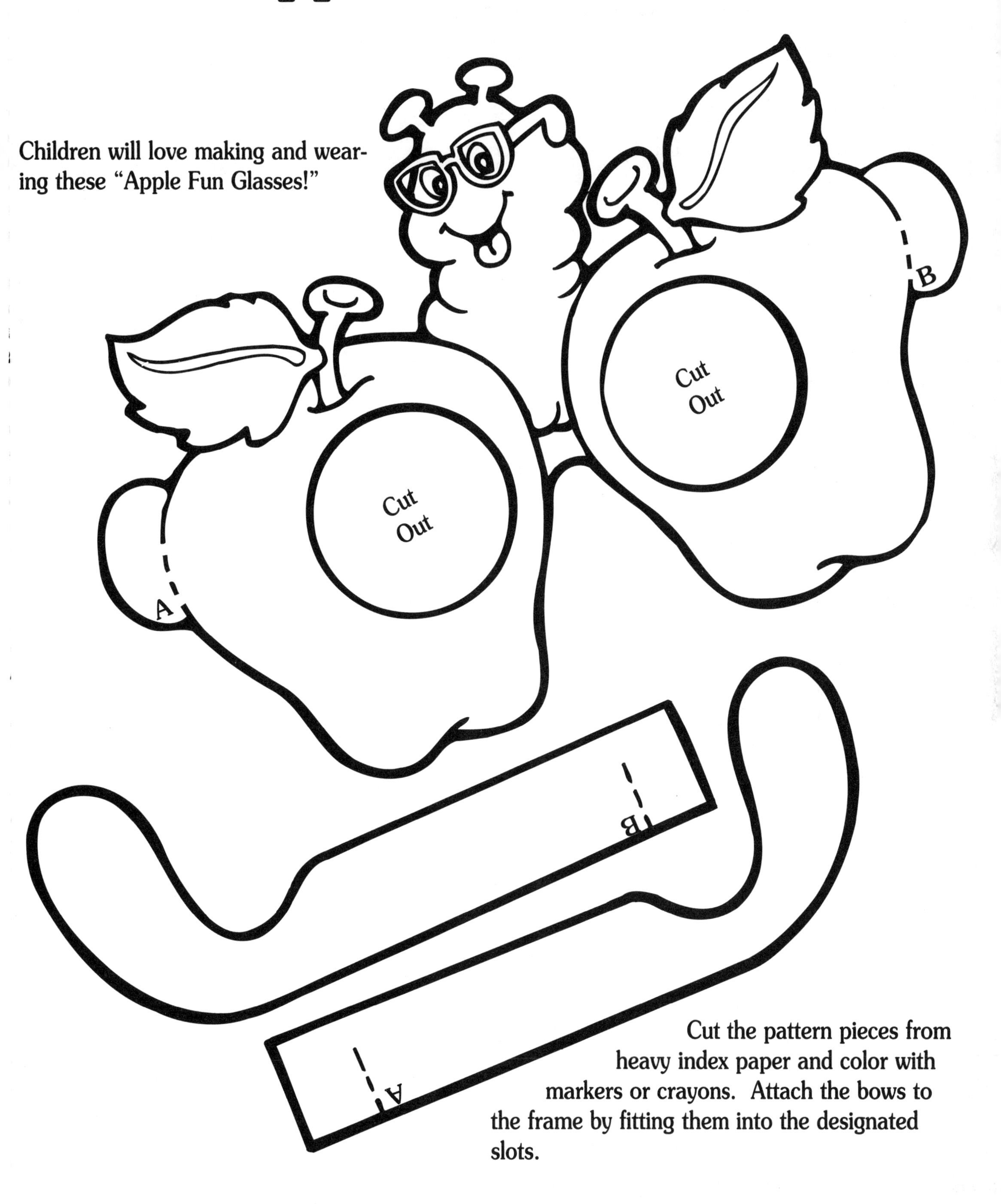

Cut the pattern pieces from heavy index paper and color with markers or crayons. Attach the bows to the frame by fitting them into the designated slots.

APPLE TIME ACTIVITIES!

APPLE TIME

Students will love sampling different types of apples in celebration of Johnny Appleseed's birthday. Introduce several different varieties to your class, such as Golden Delicious, Granny Smith, Pippin, Rome Beauty and Mackintosh. Discuss the difference of each apple in terms of color and size. Cut each apple into several pieces and have the children sample each one. Ask them to describe the taste of each apple and list descriptive words on the class chalkboard.

Write the following apple words on the class chalkboard. Have students write apple stories with many of the words or ask them to look up several of the words in the class dictionary. Children might like to use the apple pattern on page 40 for their work.

tree	graft	fruit	Delicious
stem	prune	pie	Granny Smith
core	dormant	tart	Golden
peel	orchard	Mackintosh	Pippin
branch	pistil	Jonathan	
blossom	cider	Rome	
bushel	juicy	Beauty	

With the apple pattern in this book, create your own apple task cards using these suggestions:

1. Describe how you would plant an apple tree.
2. Write five words that best describe how an apple tastes.
3. Make a list of all the things containing or made from apples.
4. Describe how you would prune an apple tree.
5. List as many words as you can using the word APPLESAUCE.
6. Describe the difference between a forest and an orchard.

Mr.
Apple

Apple Stories

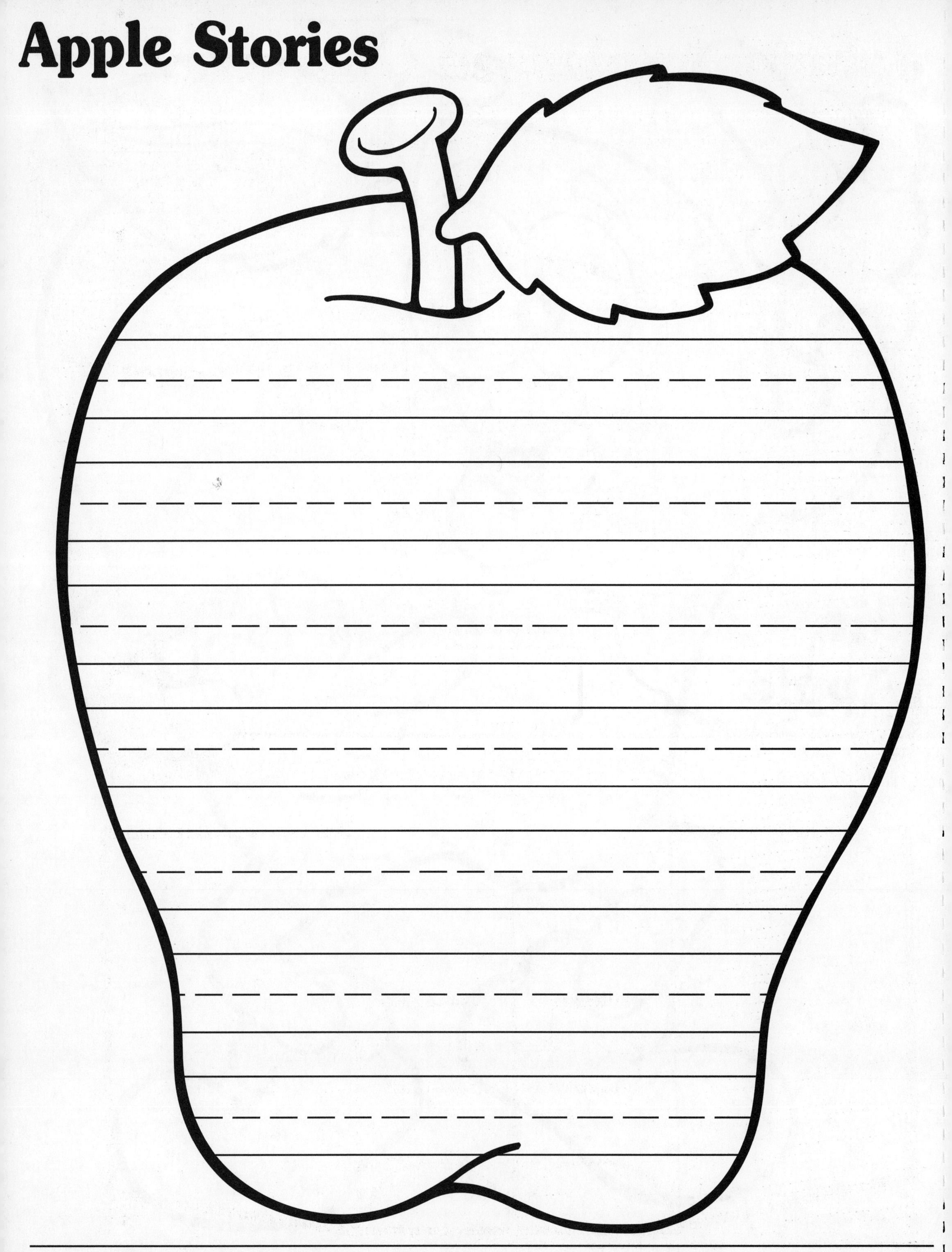

Johnny Appleseed Character

Make this cute character from index paper. Color, cut out and fold. Bend his arms forward and staple or paste the basket to his hands.

Stand-Up Worm

Cut the worm and apple pattern from heavy paper. Write your name along the worm's body and fold along the dotted lines. Glue the apple to the worm's tail. Use him as a desk nametag or a place card during family meals.

Matching Apples and Worms

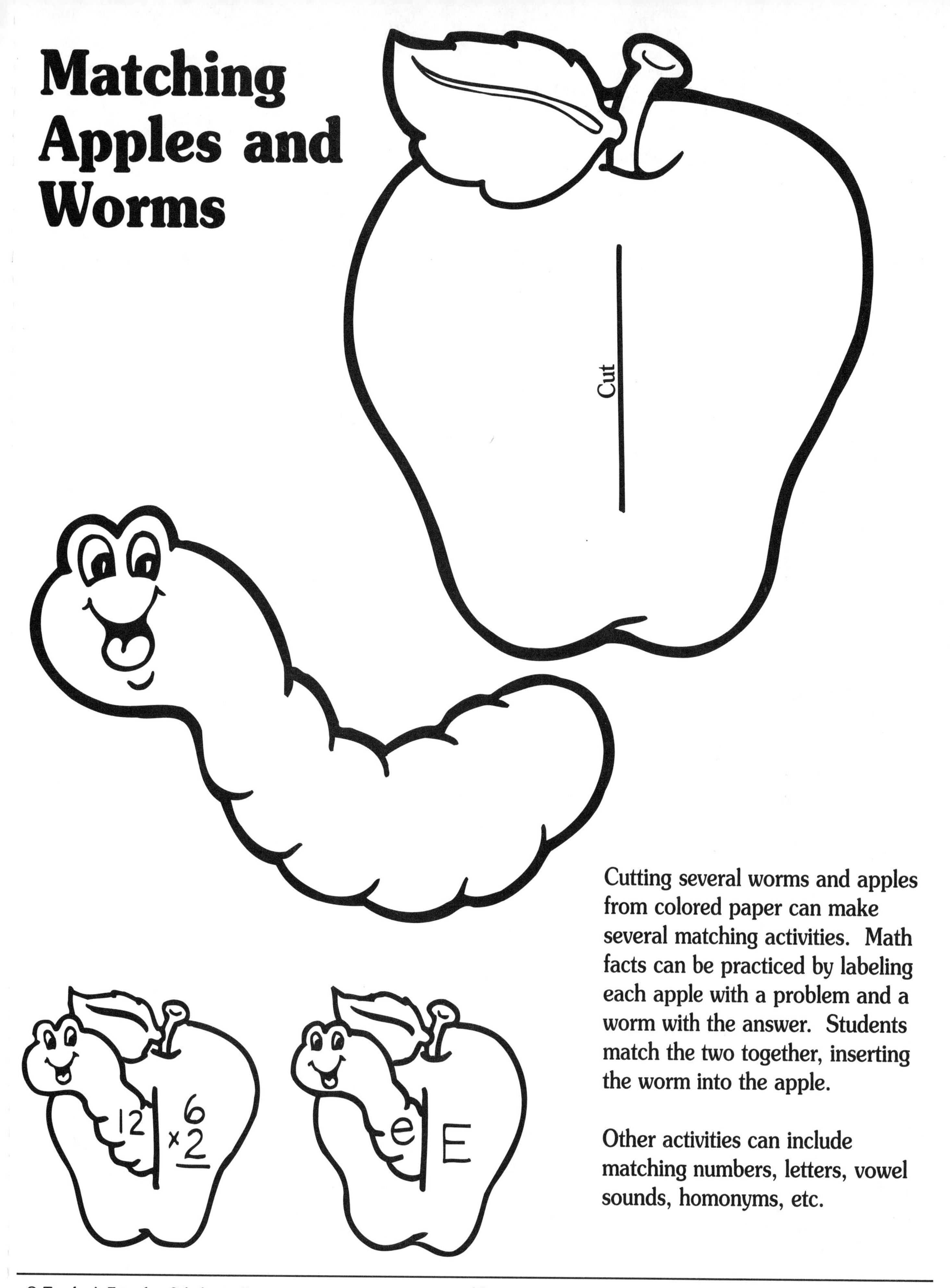

Cutting several worms and apples from colored paper can make several matching activities. Math facts can be practiced by labeling each apple with a problem and a worm with the answer. Students match the two together, inserting the worm into the apple.

Other activities can include matching numbers, letters, vowel sounds, homonyms, etc.

Apple Cores

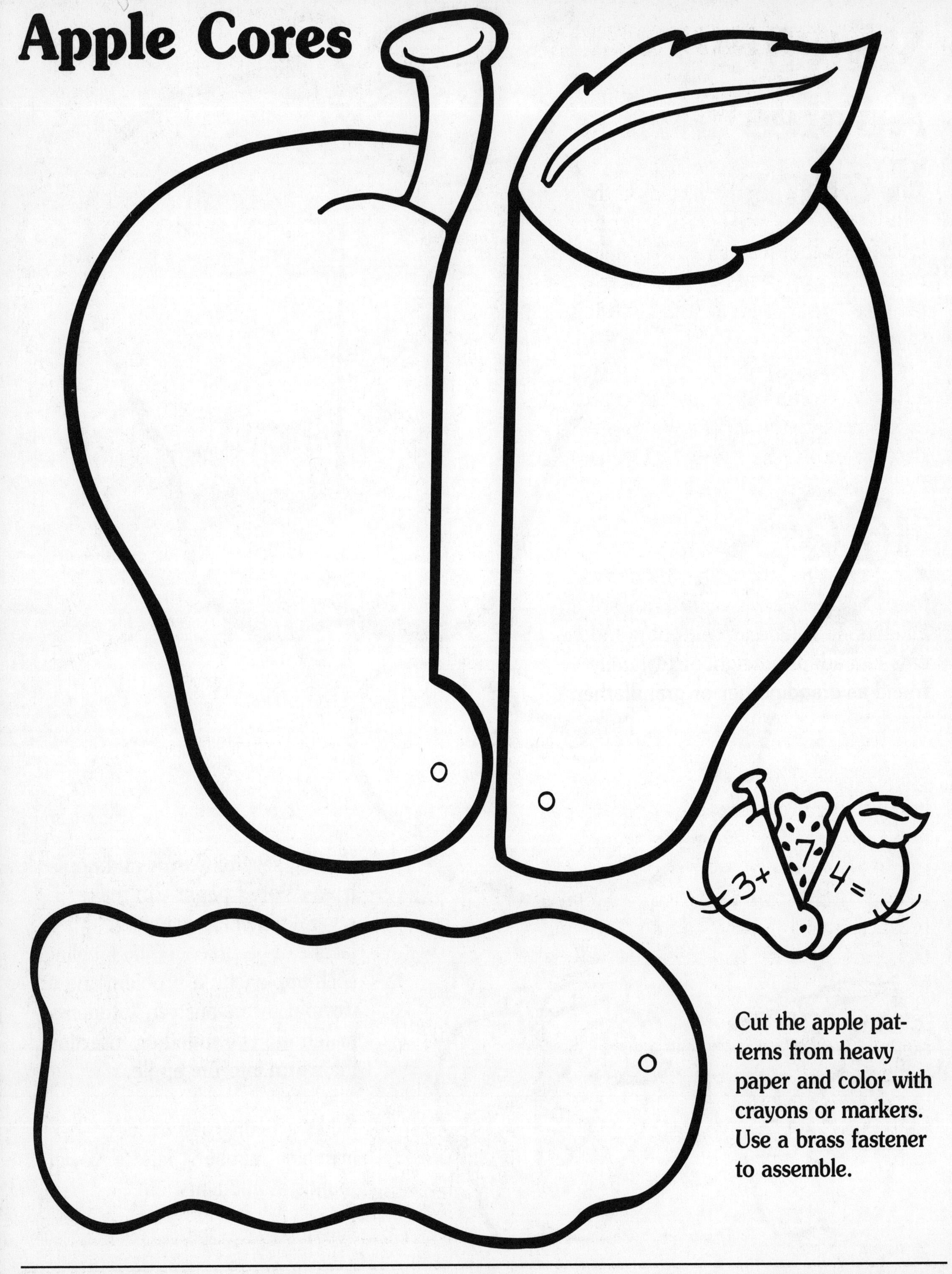

Cut the apple patterns from heavy paper and color with crayons or markers. Use a brass fastener to assemble.

Grandparent's Day

This special day is celebrated on the first Sunday after Labor Day each September. Encourage children to express their love to their grandparents and all older people with one or more of the following suggestions:

1. Ask each student to write a special message to his or her grandparent. They might like to make a card or simple gift to express their affection.

2. Have children conduct an interview with their grandparent. They might like to ask them questions about his or her childhood. (Students without grandparents can adopt a neighbor or family friend as grandmother or grandfather for the day.)

3. Arrange a visit to a local retirement home for your whole class. Children can make cards or crafts and give them to the residents that seldom get visitors. Students might like to practice singing a song and then perform it for their new friends.

Follow up with another visit before Halloween. The children can take a carved jack-o'-lantern or Halloween cookies to share.

MY GRANDFATHER!

My Grandfather is special because...

I like it when my Grandfather...

My Grandfather can do many things! I think he's best at...

My Grandfather has a great smile! I like to make him smile by...

My Grandfather is smart! He even knows...

My Grandfather is as handsome as...

Signed Date

MY GRANDMOTHER!

My Grandmother is special because... ________________

I like it when my Grandmother... ________________

My Grandmother can do many things! I think she's best at... ________________

My Grandmother has a great smile! I like to make her smile by... ________________

My Grandmother is smart! She even knows... ________________

My Grandmother is as pretty as... ________________

Signed ________________ Date ________________

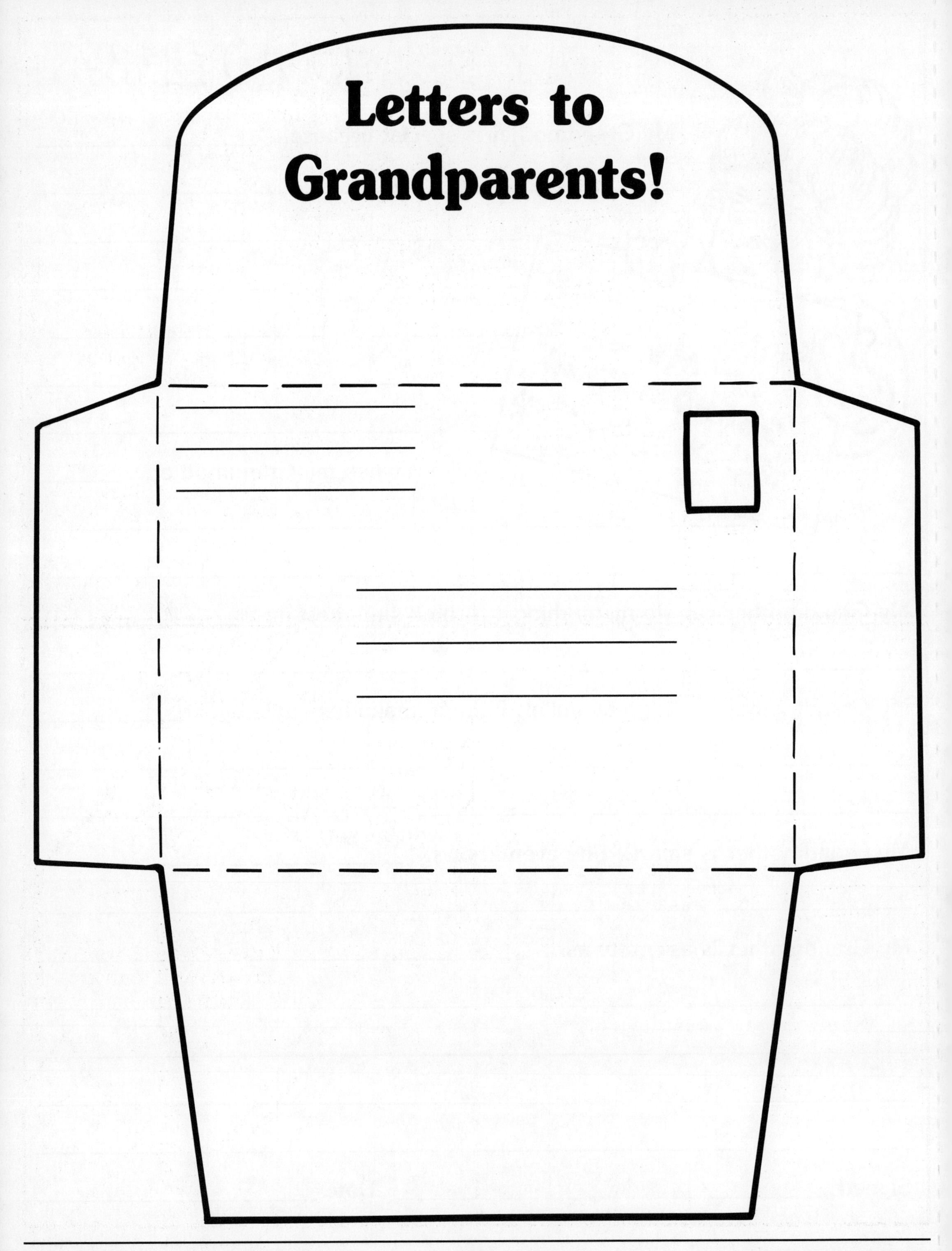
Letters to
Grandparents!

My Grandma
Paste a picture of Grandma here and write a message inside the card.
My Grandpa
Paste a picture of Grandpa here and write a message inside the card.

I'm Special Mobile!

This special mobile can easily be made by mounting each pattern piece to poster board. Color with crayons or watercolor markers. Children write their own names under "I'm Special!" They may also draw their own portrait in the framed picture. All of the pieces are assembled with string, as shown. Students can also list their favorite things on the hanging mobile pieces.

Hang the mobiles in the class windows or let students take them home to hang in their rooms.

I'm Special!!

Use these patterns with the "I'm Special!" mobile or as September nametags or calendar decorations.

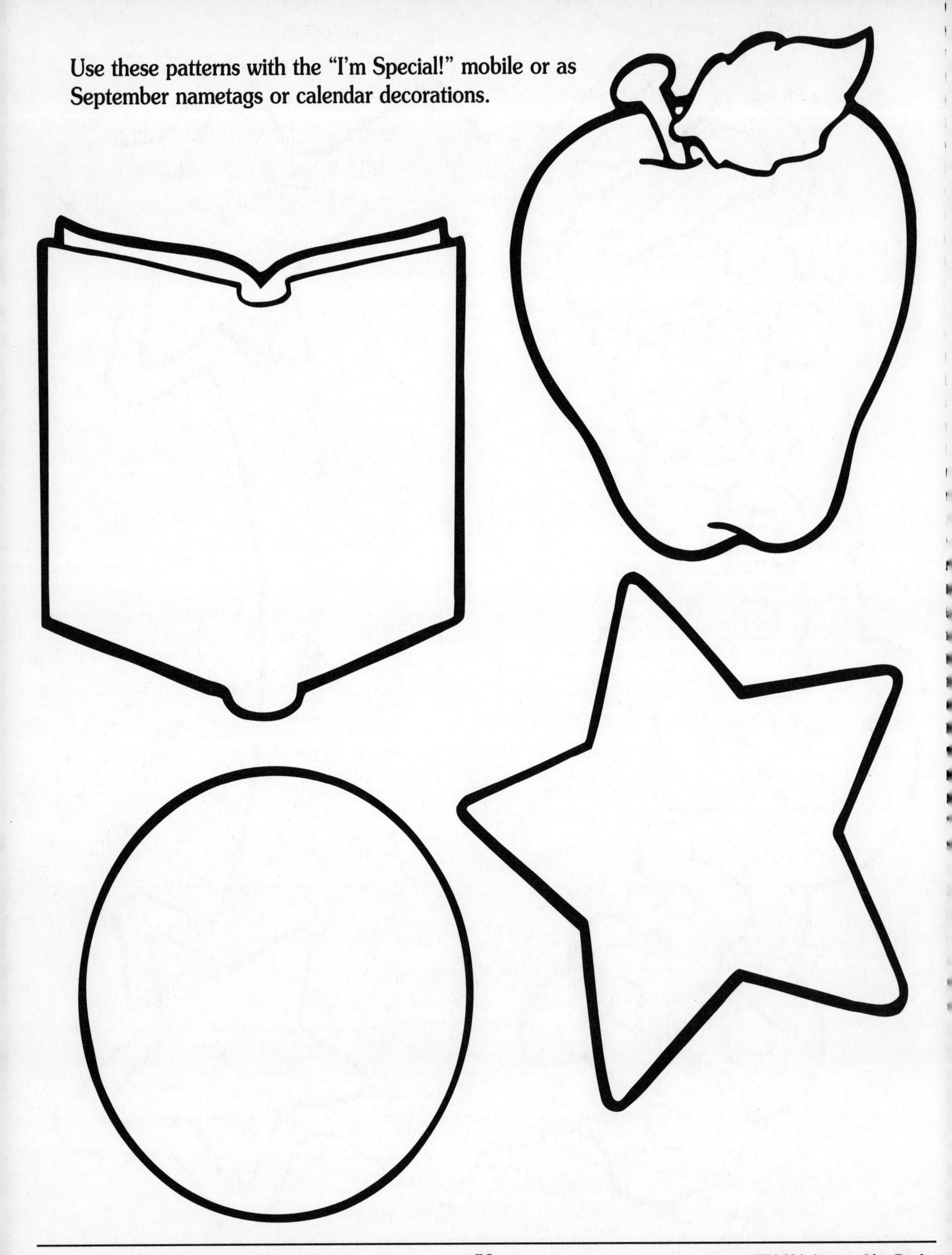

OCTOBER

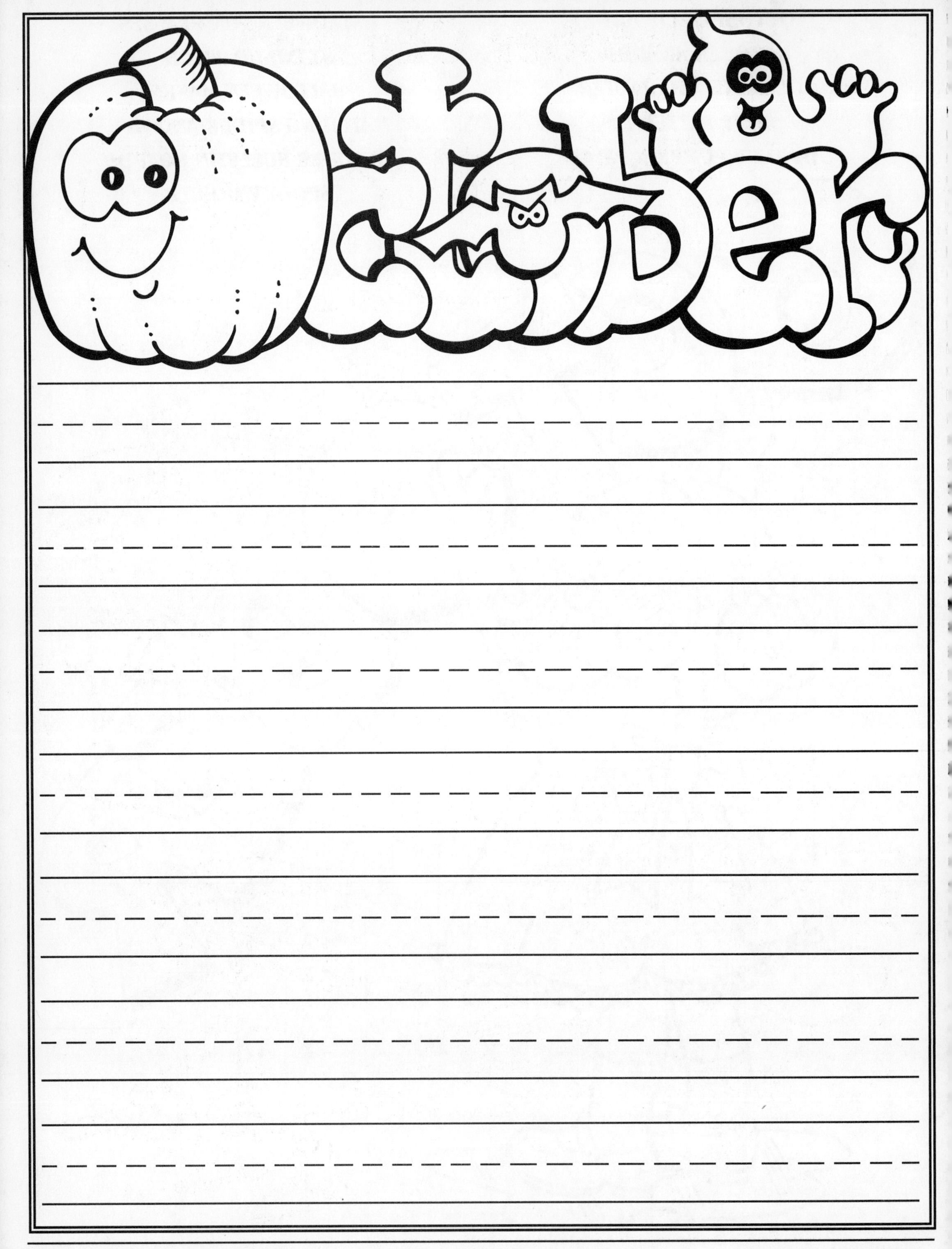
October

October Clip Art!

OCTOBER NEWSLETTER!

TEACHER:	RM# DATE:

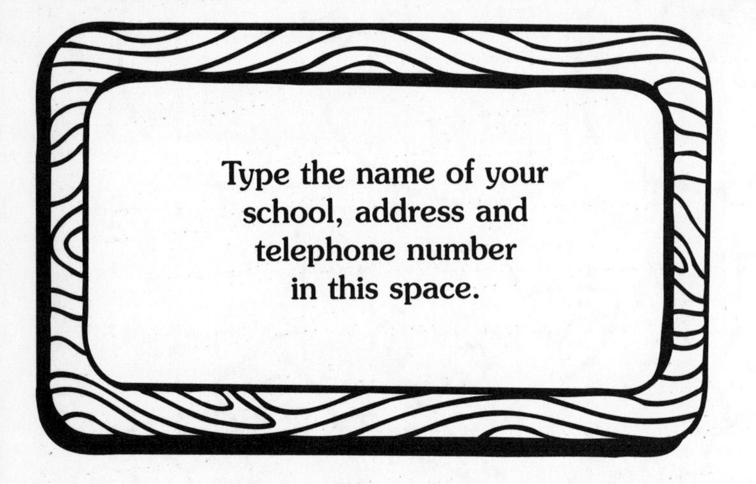

SUGGESTIONS FOR AN OCTOBER NEWSLETTER:

- List the name of each student that was selected student of the week for the month of September.
- Note the dates of Columbus Day and Halloween. Make sure that parents know which days children will not be in attendance.
- Announce special programs being conducted by your school or in your classroom.
- Tell about something special on which your class is working.
- Staple the October cafeteria menu to each newsletter.
- Ask one of your students to draw several small pictures about Halloween to be used in the October newsletter.
- Ask your school principal to write a brief message that can be included with the October newsletter.
- Ask for parent volunteers or donations for the class Halloween party.
- Announce upcoming field trips, class plays, spelling bees or fundraisers.

- Send a welcome note to a new student or a get-well message to a student that has been out ill.
- List several safety precautions that should be observed during Halloween.
- Ask each family to discuss fire prevention in observance of Fire Prevention Week.

SUPER STUDENT AWARD!

awarded to

____

for

____

____

____

____

Date

____

Teacher

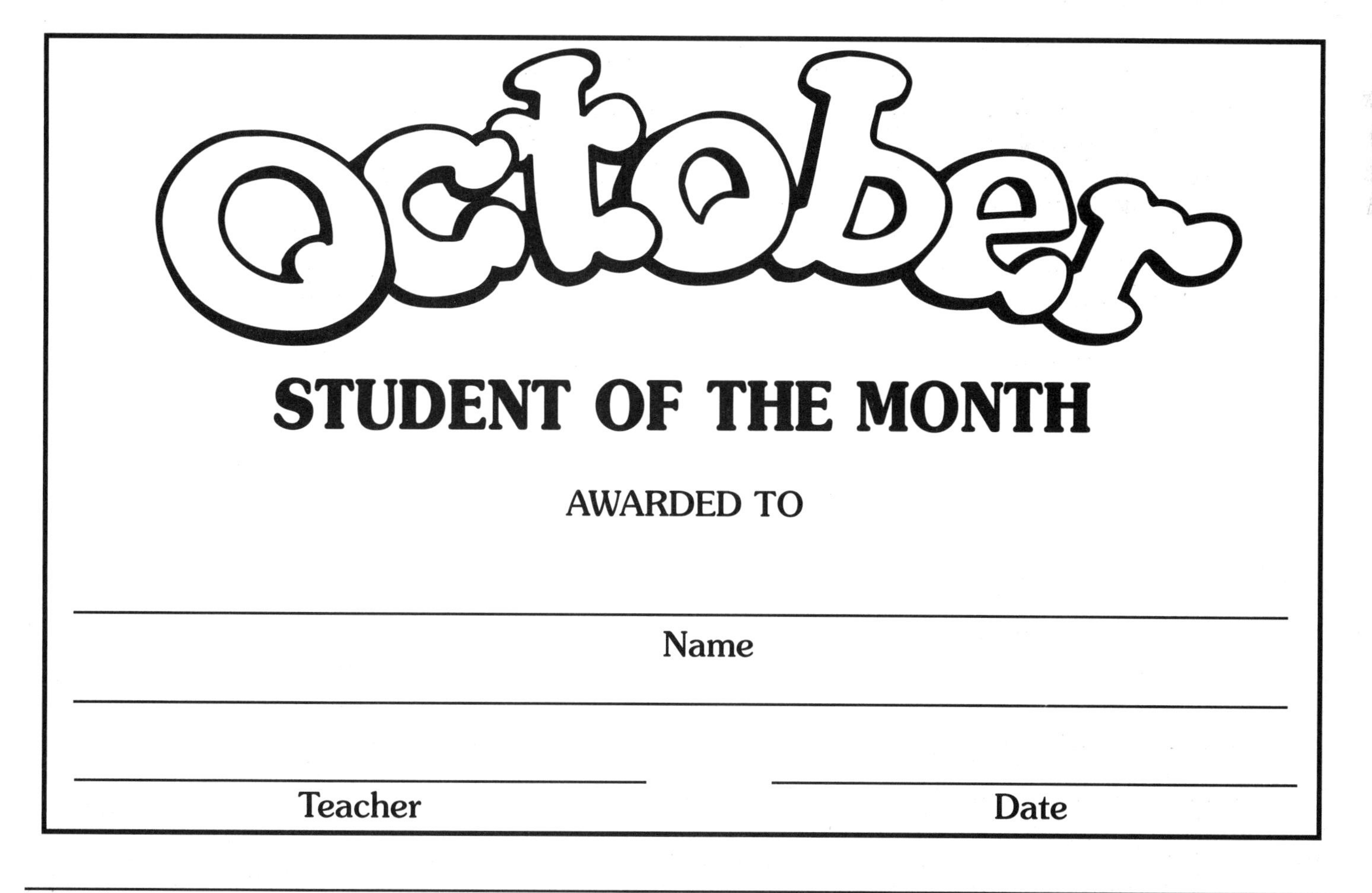
October

STUDENT OF THE MONTH

AWARDED TO

____

Name

____

______________________________ ______________________________

Teacher Date

OCTOBER FUN!

OCTOBER'S OWN

A pumpkin field's an ideal place
To visit, it has lots of space.
Ripened pumpkins lie on the ground,
Some are oval, some are round.
You can pluck one off the vine
And carve it in your own design.

FUNNY MASKS

When I put on a funny mask,
Everyone will surely ask,
"Who is that? Who can it be?"
I'll laugh and say,
"It's me! It's me!"

POPCORN

When making popcorn, you'll discover
The pan you use will need a cover.
No cover? Then you'll need a broom.
Popcorn will fly all over the room.
Quickly you will understand
Kernels heated soon expand.
Crunchy popcorn is delicious.
Since it's corn, it is nutritious!

OCTOBER IS NATIONAL POPCORN MONTH!

CREATE A WITCH!

Ask students to close their eyes and imagine the face of a witch. Have them make a list of her features on a piece of paper. They should list such things as teeth, hair, nose, eyes, mouth, skin, etc. Each student should then select an adjective descriptive for each feature and write it down. One description might be "evil eyes, crooked smile, twisted nose, spiked hair and green skin."

After students have created a verbal witch, ask them to create a visual one. Suggest that each child draw a detailed picture of the witch they've described. The best witches along with their descriptions can be posted on the class bulletin board.

Stand-Up Witch!

Make this cute witch character from index paper. Color, cut out and fold. Bend her arms forward and staple or paste the broom to her hands.

Use her as a Halloween centerpiece.

Flipped-Out Pumpkin!

Younger students will enjoy making this pumpkin that "flips its lid!" Cut the pumpkin from orange paper and assemble with a brass fastener. Students can draw their own faces on the pumpkin.

Stand-Up Pumpkin Patch!

Cut out the ghost and pumpkins from heavy paper. Draw your own jack-o'-lantern faces on the pumpkins. Fan fold along the dotted lines. Glue the ghost to the first pumpkin and stand on a desk top for a "spooky" decoration.

Halloween Fun Glasses!

Children will love making and wearing these "Halloween Fun Glasses" on October 31st!

Cut the pattern pieces from heavy index paper and color with markers or crayons. Attach the bows to the frame by fitting them into the designated slots.

Columbus Character!

Make the Christopher Columbus character from index paper. Color, cut and fold. Attach the spyglass to his right hand. Stand on a table for a special Columbus Day decoration.

Ship Pattern!

Make three ships and label them the Nina, Pinta and Santa Maria.

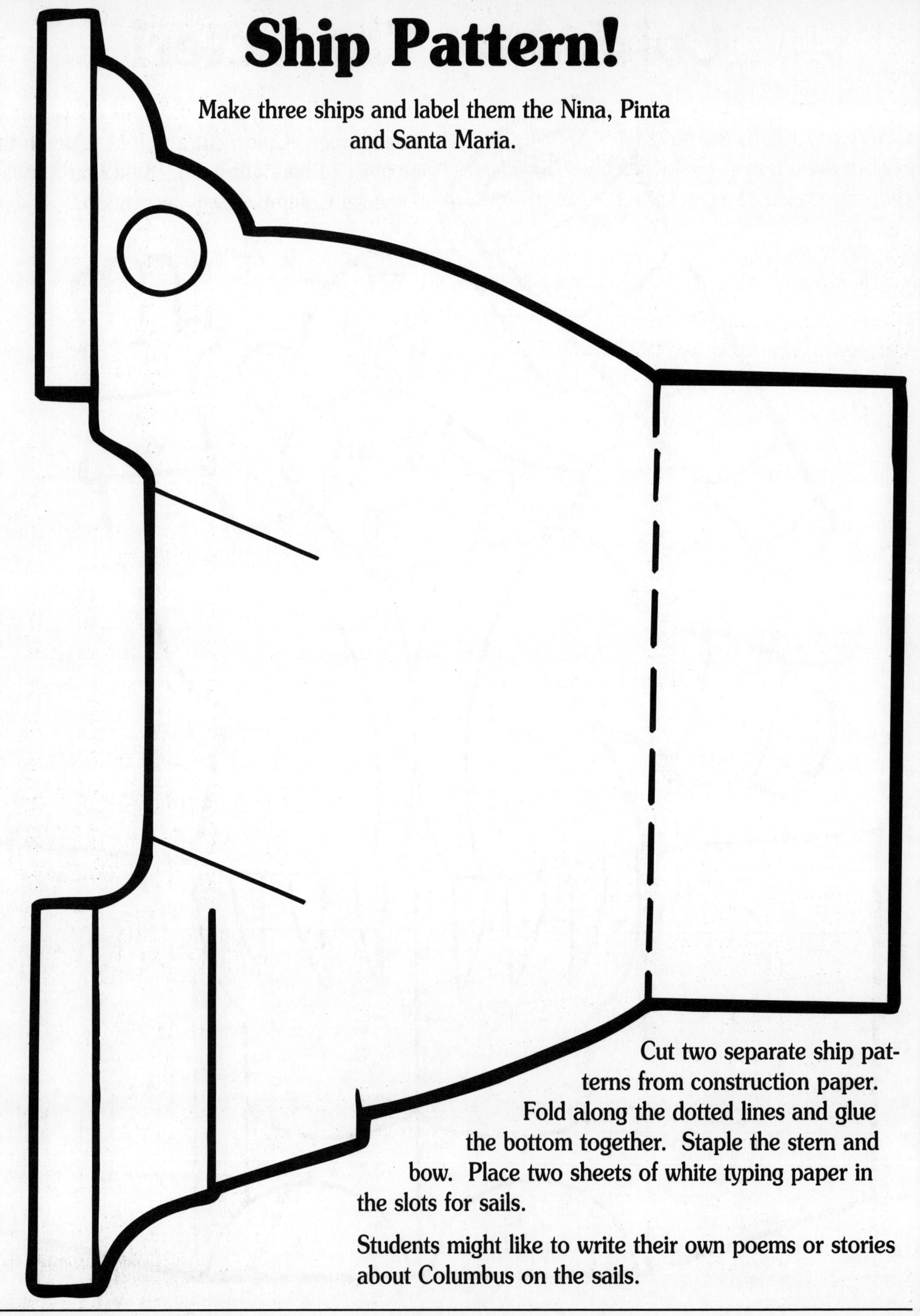

Cut two separate ship patterns from construction paper. Fold along the dotted lines and glue the bottom together. Staple the stern and bow. Place two sheets of white typing paper in the slots for sails.

Students might like to write their own poems or stories about Columbus on the sails.

HALLOWEEN MASK PATTERNS!

Children will love making their own masks for Halloween using these mask patterns. Each mask can be made in several different ways.

TIE-ON MASKS

Mask patterns can be copied onto colored paper and pasted to tag board or poster board. Cut out the eye openings and attach kite string to both sides. Tie the string behind the child's head to hold it in place.

STICK MASKS

These mask patterns can also be attached to a tongue depressor or Popsicle stick. Cut the mask from poster board and simply tape the stick to the back of the mask. The child holds the mask in front of his or her face.

PAPER BAG MASKS

Paper bag masks can also be made with these mask patterns. Cut each mask from colored paper and paste it to a medium or large grocery bag. Cut out the eye openings and a small opening at the mouth for the child to easily breathe. Try these other ideas:

- Fringed paper can be added for a lion's mane.
- Paper feathers can be made into a collar for an owl costume.
- Pipe cleaner whiskers can be added to several mask patterns.

Lion Mask

Bear Mask

Cut
Out

Cut
Out

Owl Mask

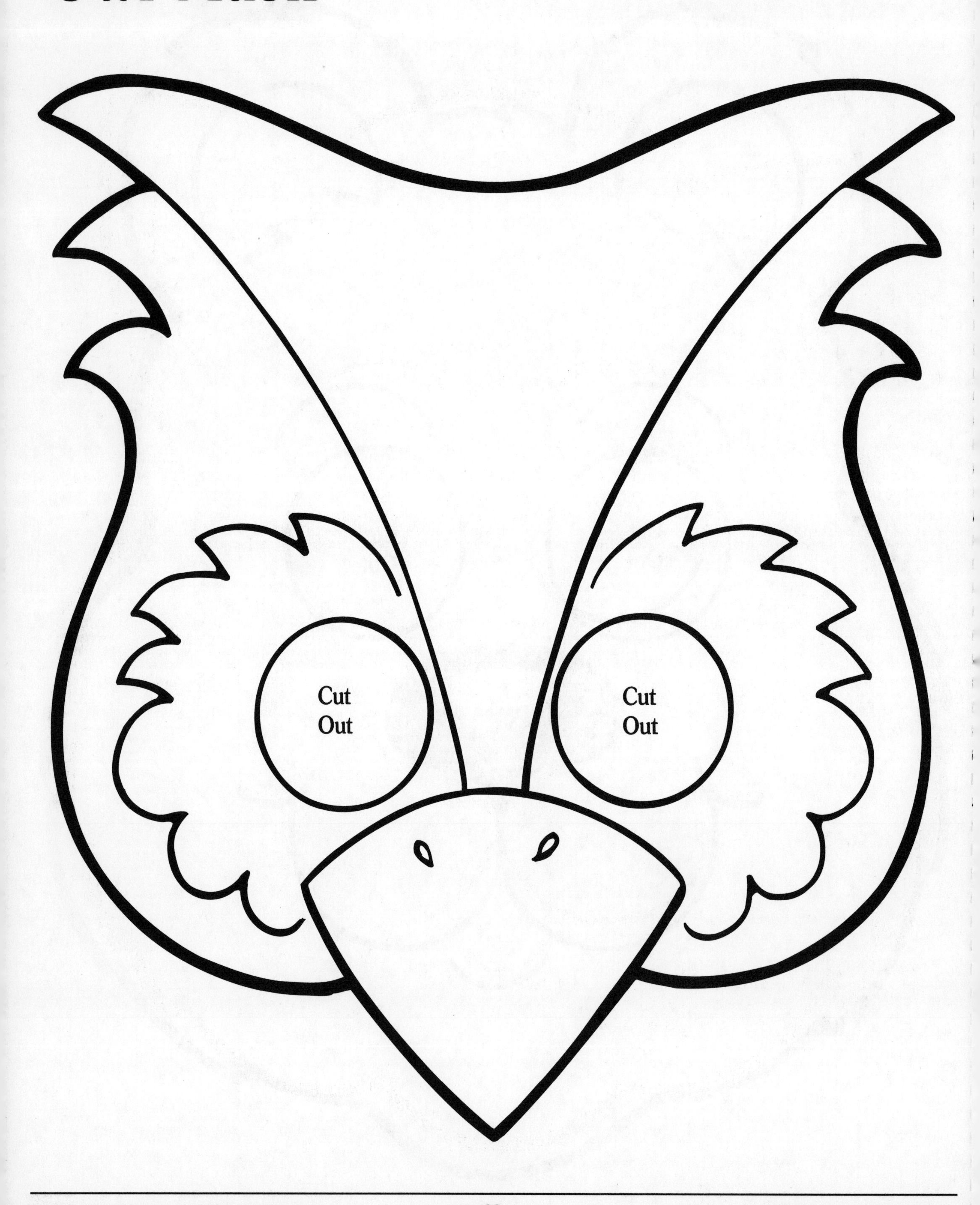

Cat Mask

Matching Spider and Web!

Cutting several spiders and webs from colored paper can make many matching activities.

Write a question on the spider and the answer on the web. Students match the two together to solve the problem.

Four-Sided Pumpkin!

Make this easy party favor from orange construction paper. Draw a different face on each side. Fold at the dotted lines and staple the opposite stems together. Stand him on a table as a name card or fill him with Halloween candy.

OCTOBER BULLETIN BOARDS!

HARVEST TIME!
Inspire young writers with this October pumpkin patch. Have each student write spooky stories on large paper pumpkins. Display them on the class bulletin board along with stalks of corn, a picket fence and a paper harvest moon. Use dark blue or black paper for the background to create a midnight effect.

POP TO IT!
Children love popcorn! Make popcorn in the classroom and then have each child write about the experience on large paper kernels. Display the best papers on the class board.

You may like to glue popcorn kernels to poster board to form the word POP!

WHAT'S COOKING?
Ask students to use their math and writing skills to write creative recipes.

Using the Halloween theme, have them write recipes for a magic potion or a witch's brew on large circles of cut paper. Arrange the "bubbles" on the class bulletin board along with a witch stirring her pot, as shown.

Pumpkin Stories!

Write a spooky Halloween story.

Write your ideas
about popcorn using this
patterns as a booklet cover.

Witch's Brew!

Spooky Mobile!

Each child can make his or her own "spooky" mobile by cutting these patterns from construction paper. Hang the patterns using kite string or heavy thread.

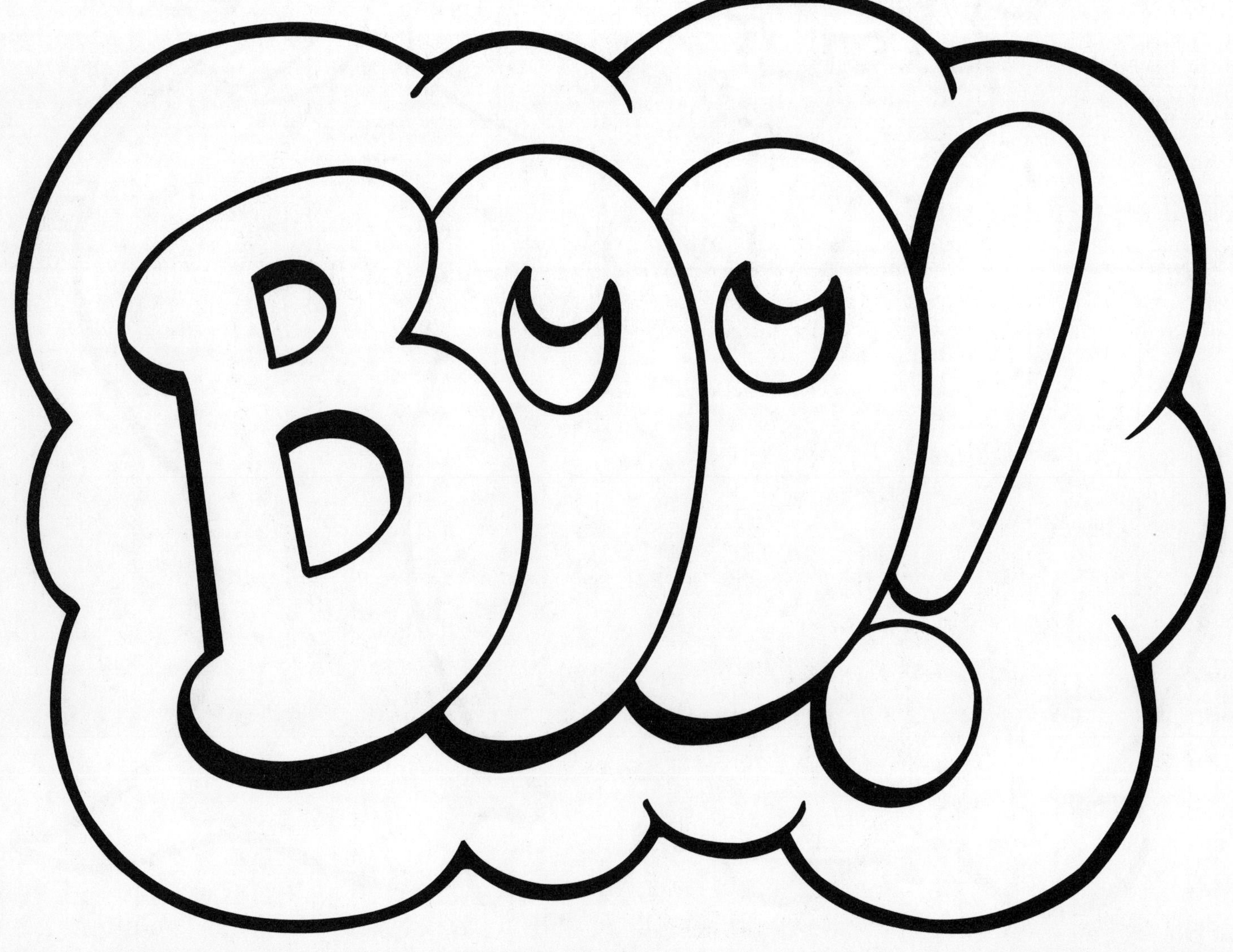

NOVEMBER

November

November Clip Art!

NOVEMBER NEWSLETTER!

TEACHER:	RM# DATE:

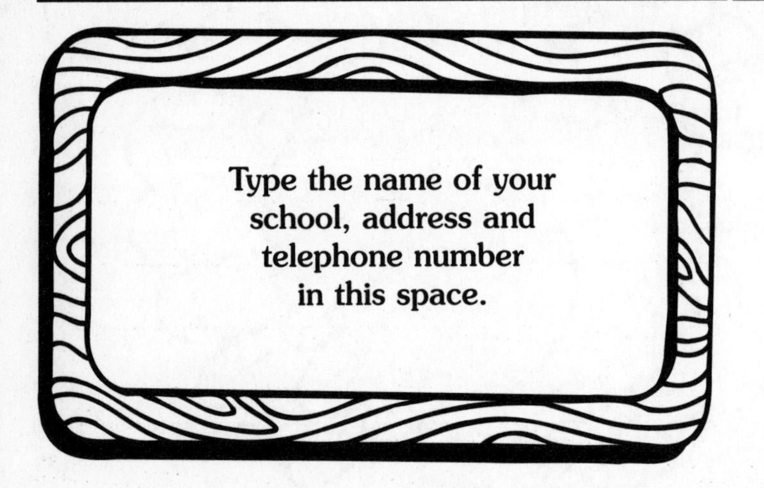

SUGGESTIONS FOR A NOVEMBER NEWSLETTER:

- List the name of each student that was selected student of the week for the month of October.
- Note the dates of Veteran's Day and the Thanksgiving holiday. Make sure that parents know which days children will not be in attendance.
- List parent conference days and include necessary information.
- Remind parents of Election Day and ask them to set a good example for their children and vote!

- Announce special programs being conducted by your school or in your classroom.
- Tell about something special on which your class is working.
- Emphasize your classroom rules or homework policy.
- Staple the November cafeteria menu to each newsletter.
- Ask one of your students to draw several small pictures about Thanksgiving to be used in the November newsletter.

- Ask your school principal to write a brief message that can be included with the November newsletter.
- Ask for parent volunteers or donations.
- Announce upcoming field trips, class plays, spelling bees or fund raisers.
- Send a welcome note to a new student or a get-well message to a student that has been out ill.

SUPER STUDENT AWARD!

awarded to

for

Date

Teacher

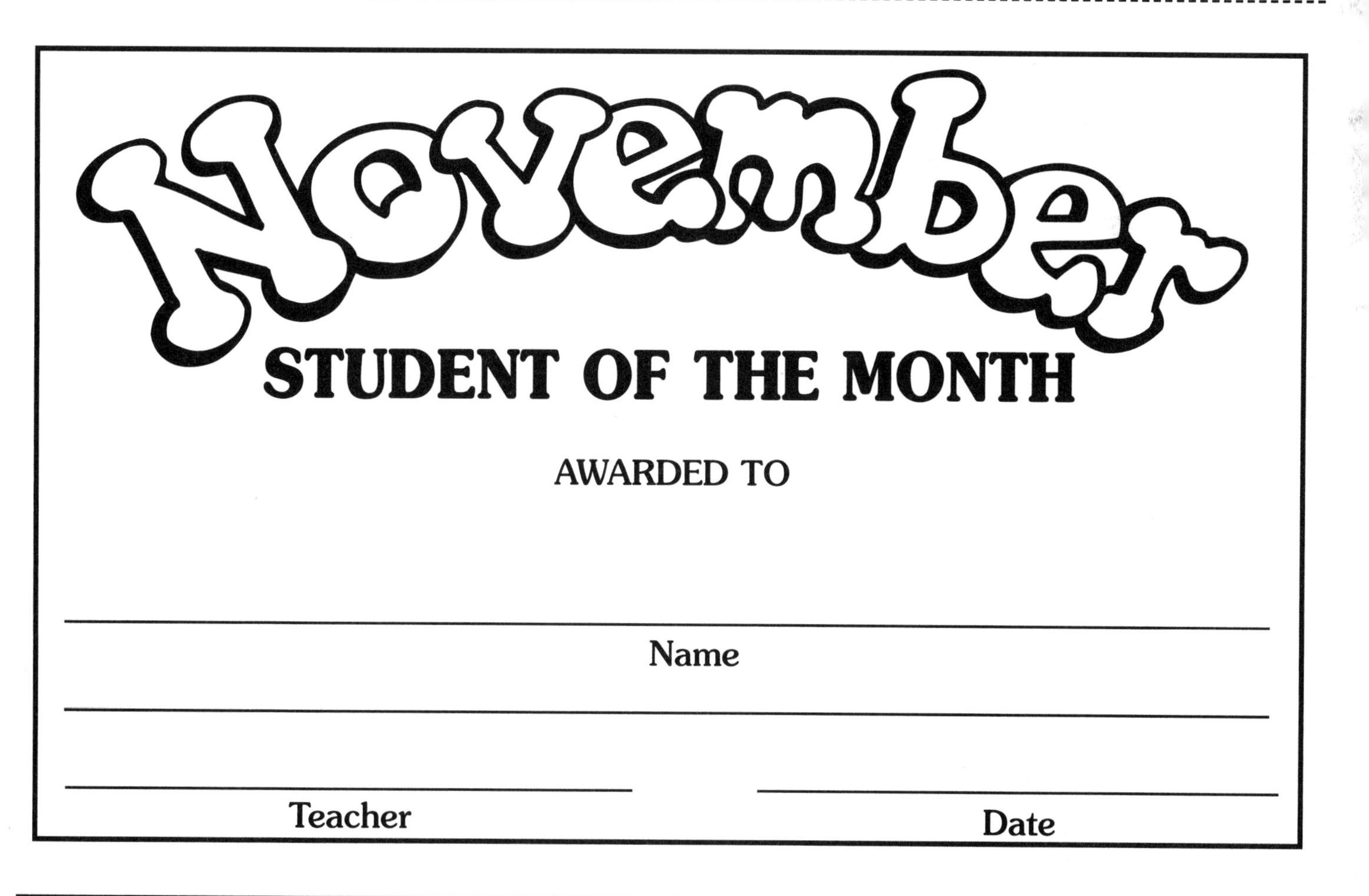

TURKEY TIME!

TURKEY STUFF!

All turkeys have a hollow space.
In there, the dressing you can place.
The dressing's made of hard, dry bread
Or cracker crumbs are used instead.

A tiny bit of water will do
And salt and pepper and you're through.
Push gently all this mix inside
As if all this you want to hide.

Stuff the turkey plump and fat.
A turkey looks quite good like that.
Sew up the hole with string or thread.
It won't hurt him, he's mighty dead.

We stuff the turkey to the brim.
The stuffing looks real good on him.
We stuff ourselves with pie and such
And all of us may eat too much.

The turkey looks like he will split,
So good I ate too much of it.
Now, I'm afraid that I will burst
And I thought he would do it first.

I should have stopped when I'd had enough.
Now, I'm the one who's overstuffed!

Try one of these Thanksgiving activities:

- Have students create an alphabet dinner by asking them to write the names of food that they might have for a Thanksgiving dinner using each letter of the alphabet. An example might be:

  A – Apple Pie
  B – Biscuits
  C – Cranberry Sauce

- Students will express a renewed interest in math by creating Thanksgiving math problems and then solving them Select a few students to plan a Thanksgiving menu and add up the cost of an actual meal. Others can calculate how many people will be attending and figure the number of chairs, forks, knives, etc. that will be needed.

Turkey Napkin Ring!

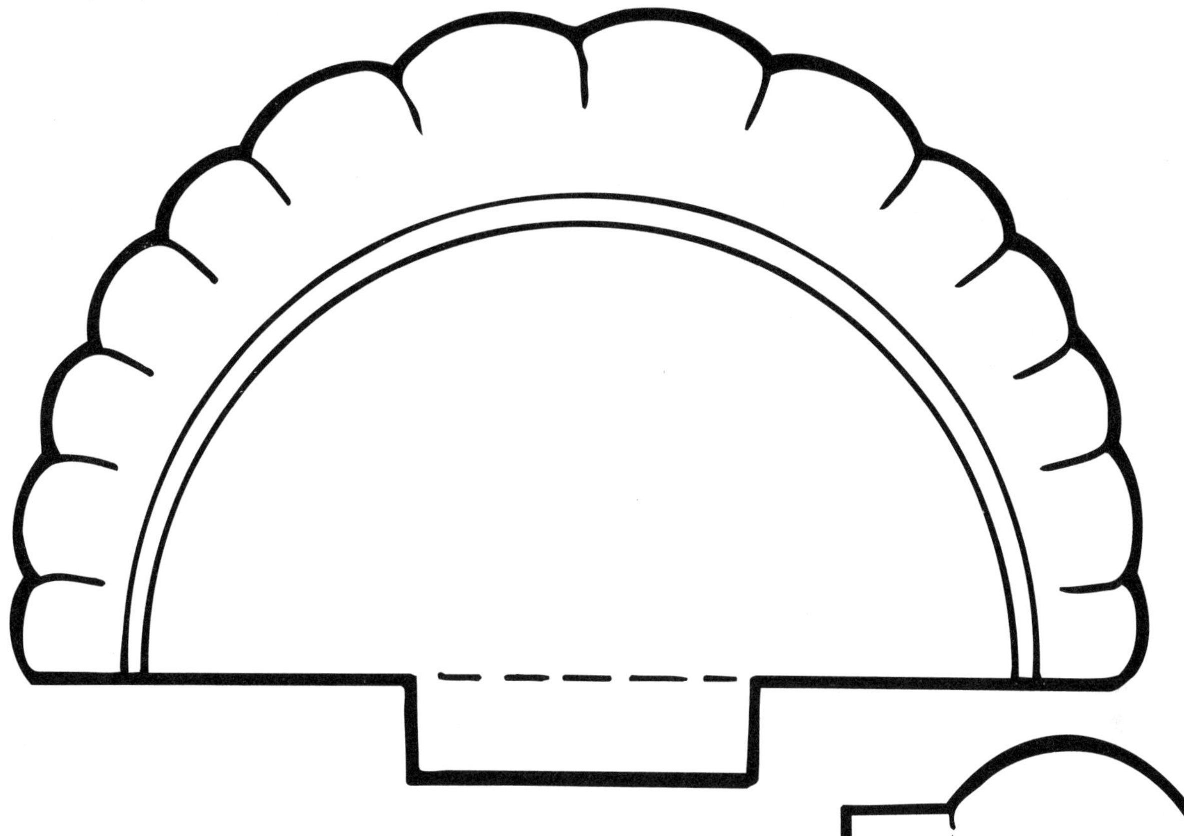

Make this simple turkey Napkin Ring and Name Place Card from construction paper. Cut one strip of paper 2" X 9" and staple together to form a loop. Cut out the turkey head and tail and glue into place, as shown. Paste the turkey to a square of poster board. Roll a paper napkin and place it in the loop.

Children will love making this cute turkey decoration for everyone in the family.

November Fun Glasses!

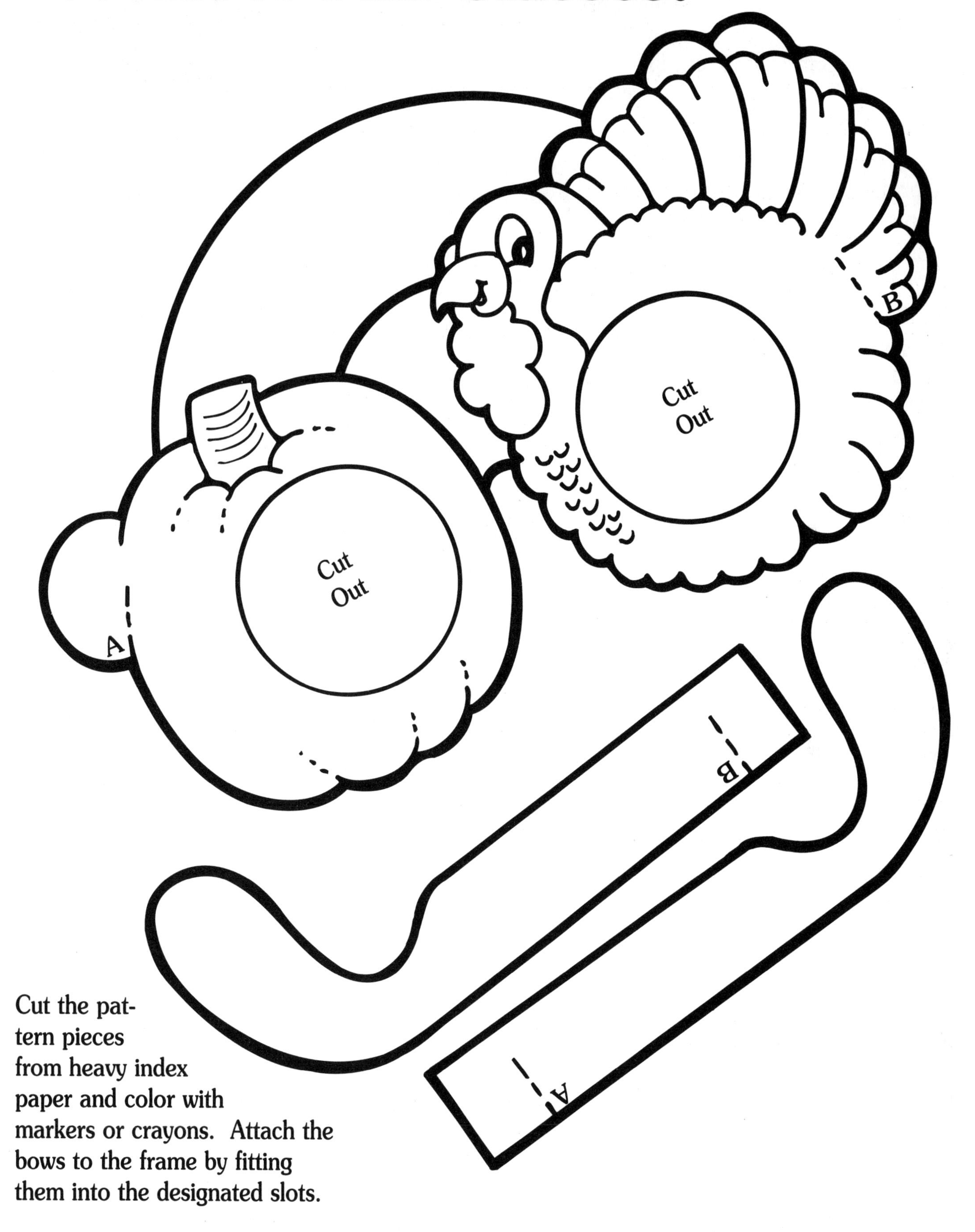

Cut the pattern pieces from heavy index paper and color with markers or crayons. Attach the bows to the frame by fitting them into the designated slots.

Thanksgiving Characters!

Copy these cute "Thanksgiving Characters" onto construction paper and cut them out.

Color the characters with crayons or colored markers. Bend the arms forward and staple or paste their Thanksgiving contribution to their hands. Fold the lower half along the dotted lines toward the back to make the characters stand.

These Pilgrim and Indian characters can be used as place cards for the family's Thanksgiving dinner.

Children can also have fun making a Thanksgiving centerpiece by arranging the characters in a circle. Face each character out and staple their hands together.

Students might like to use the characters to illustrate the story of the first Thanksgiving.

Creative Writing Turkeys!

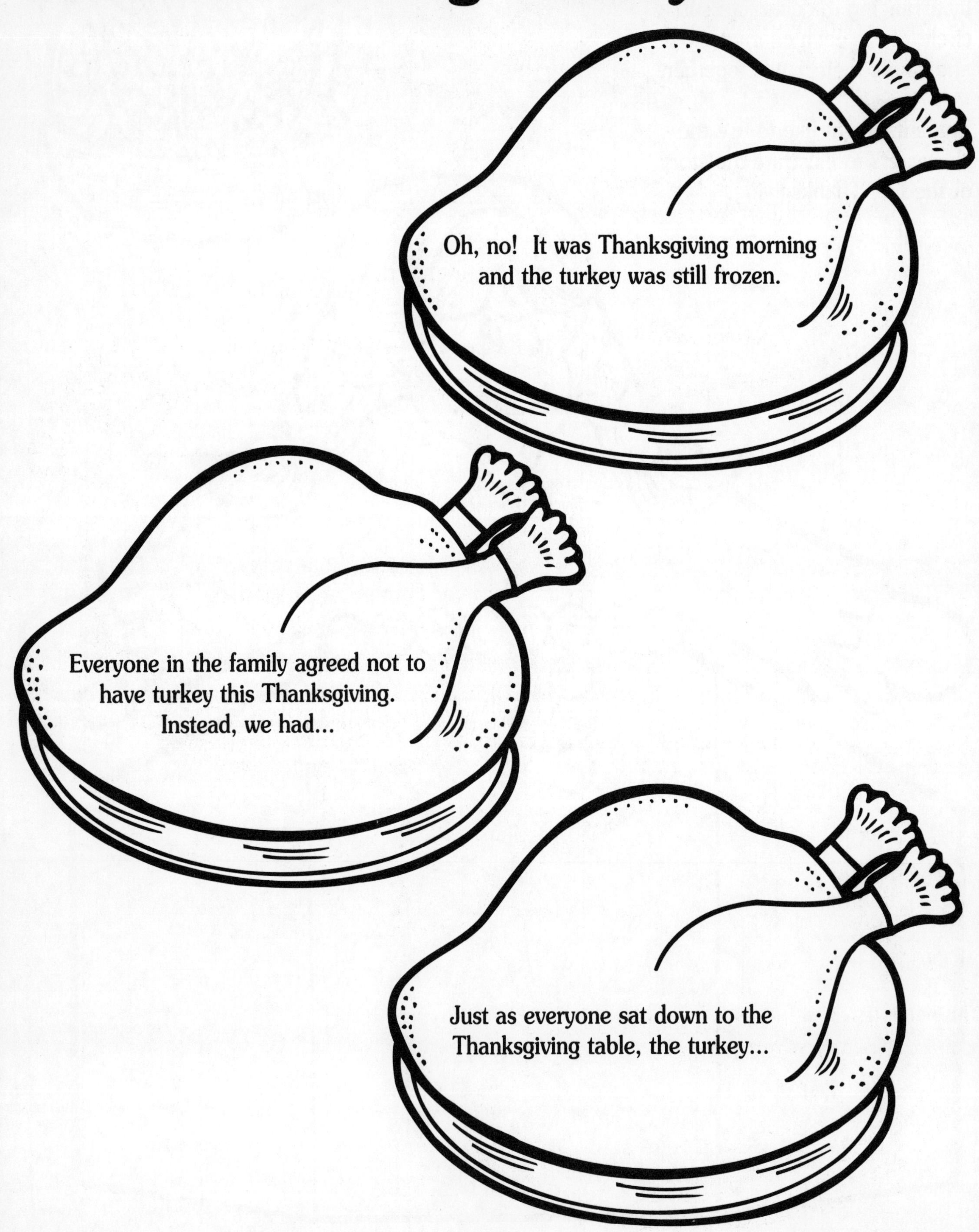

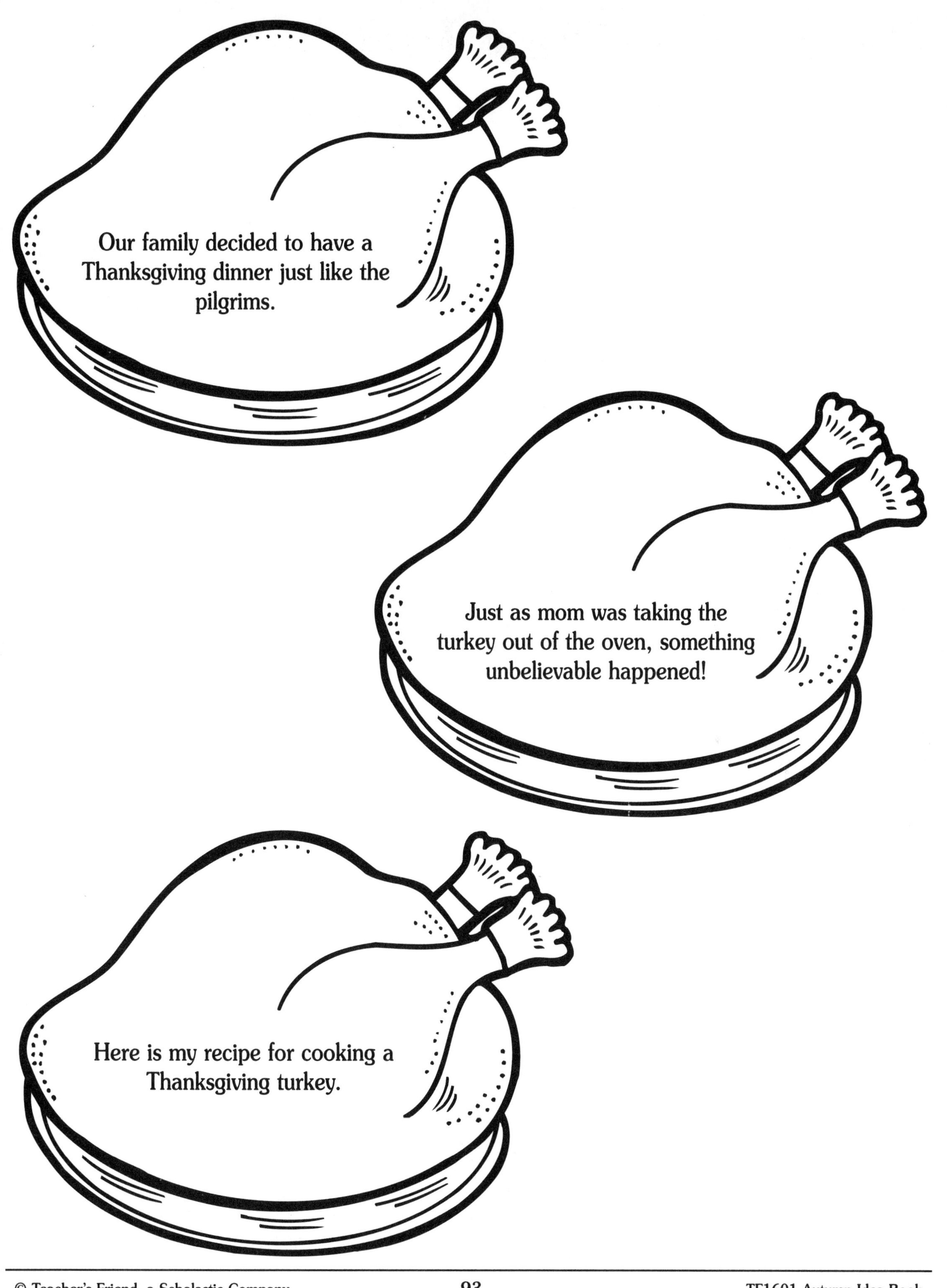
Our family decided to have a
Thanksgiving dinner just like the
pilgrims.
Just as mom was taking the
turkey out of the oven, something
unbelievable happened!
Here is my recipe for cooking a
Thanksgiving turkey.

Matching Squirrel and Nuts!

Cut several squirrels and nuts from colored construction paper to make a variety of matching activities.

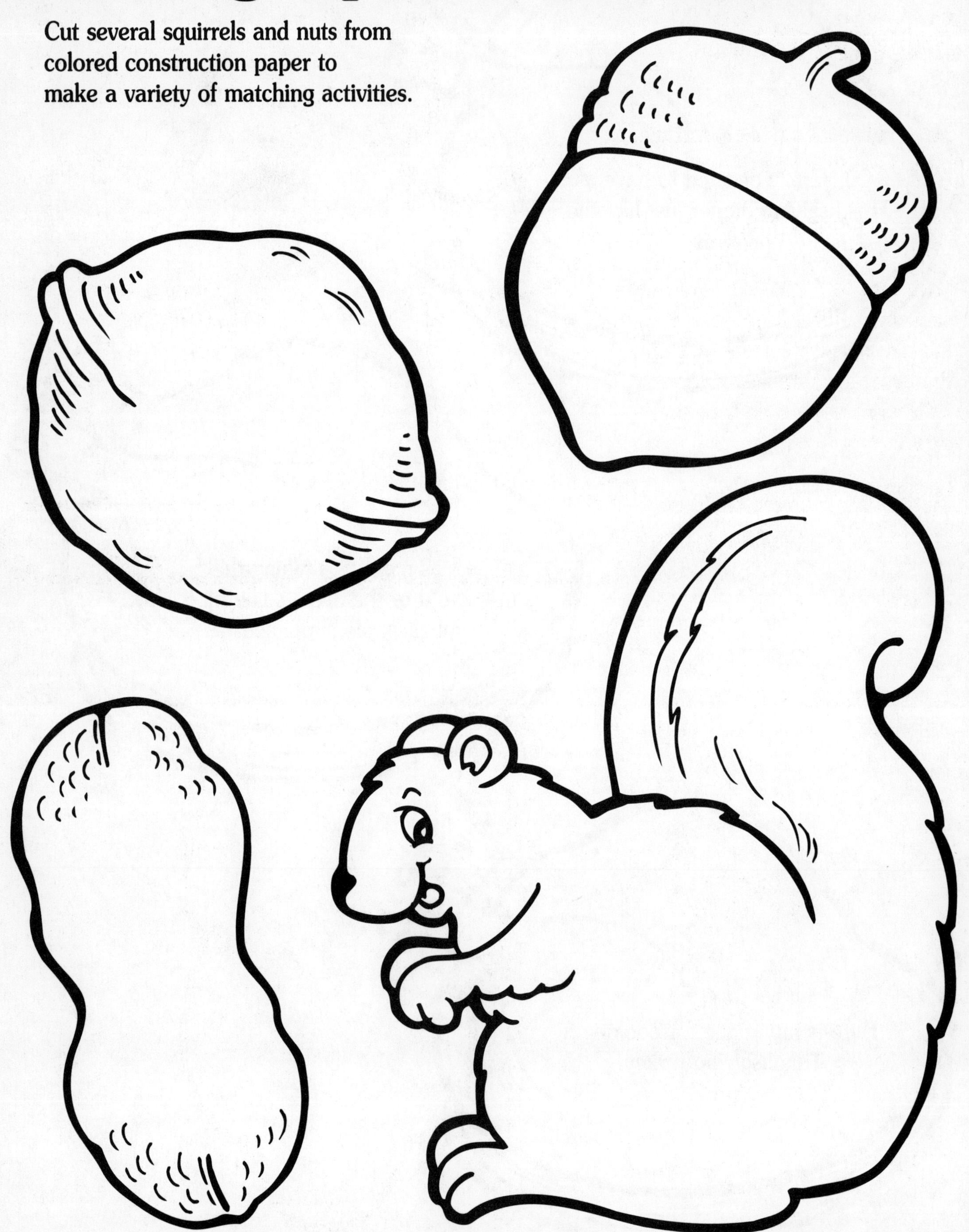

Stand-Up Squirrel!

Make this cute squirrel craft using brown construction paper.

Cut out the squirrel pattern and color with crayons. Fold his arms and legs forward. Fold the squirrel's tail back and curl it around a pencil. Paste or staple the acorn to his arms. Stand your squirrel on a desk or table-top.

This squirrel pattern could also be used as a name place card.

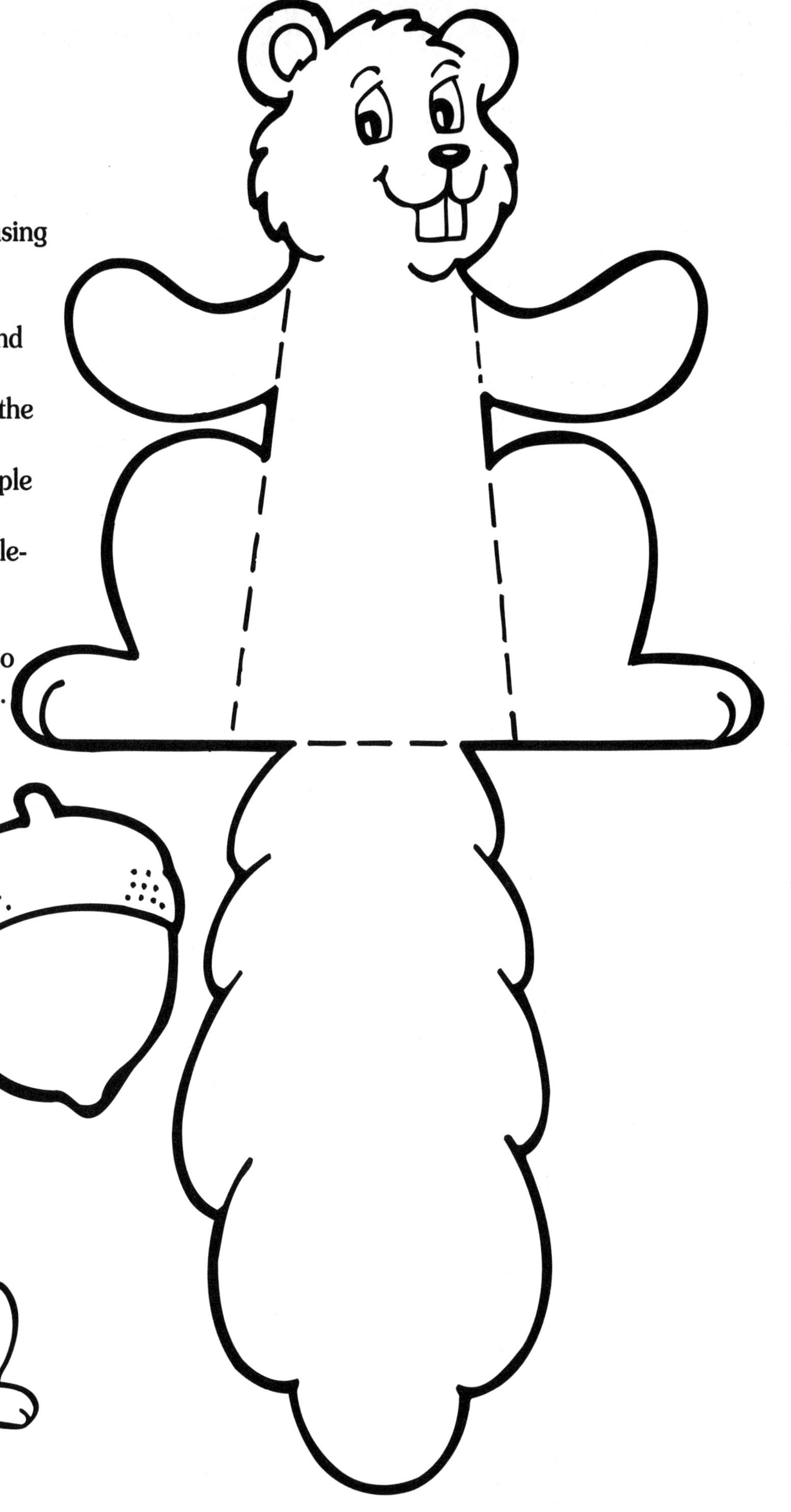

NOVEMBER BULLETIN BOARDS!

THANKFUL CORNUCOPIA
Display a large cornucopia on the class bulletin board. Write each student's name on a folded piece of construction paper and ask him or her to list what he or she is most grateful for inside. Pin these to the inside of the cornucopia, as shown.

3-D TURKEY!
Cut three large circles and the turkey pattern from fall colored poster board. Cut a sponge into several small pieces and glue the pieces between the layers of the turkey. Let dry overnight. In the morning, pin the three-dimensional turkey to the class bulletin board and have students display their best work papers on each side.

PIECE OF PIE
This is a great way to demonstrate fractions to your students! Display several large "pumpkin pies" on the class board, each representing different fractions. Children can take a piece of pie and announce to the class how much of the pie is left. At the conclusion of the activity, make a pumpkin pie in class for everyone to enjoy!

Enlarge the cornucopia for the class bulletin board. Place the name of each student in the opening of the "horn of plenty."

Turkey Pattern!

FOOTBALL ACTIVITIES

FOOTBALL PLAYER

CHEERLEADER

FOOTBALL FEVER GAME

FOOTBALL CHARACTERS

CREATIVE WRITING FOOTBALLS

FOOTBALL BOOKLET

FOOTBALL BULLETIN BOARDS

Football

A football field is long and wide
With husky players on each side.
The quarterback's an important man.
He runs with the ball as fast as he can.
His teammates give him close protection.
He'd never run in the wrong direction.
But if he did and that player was you,
Besides saying "Oops," what would you do?

Try these football activities:

SPORTSWRITER

Watch a football game on television taking notes about the highlights of the game. Write a brief description of the two teams, team members and the most exciting moments of the game. You might want to read your news story to the class, acting like a sportscaster.

CREATE A TEAM

Make up a name for an imaginary team and decide from what city they might originate.

Choose their colors, mascot, uniform design, etc. Write a paper describing your new team and include a drawing of one of the players in full uniform.

GOOD SPORTS

List three rules of good sportsmanship pertaining to the game of football. You might also want to list three rules of good sportsmanship for the fans, as well.

FOOTBALL BINGO!

This game offers an exciting way to introduce students to football vocabulary words. Give each child a copy of the bingo words listed below or write the words on the chalkboard. Ask students to write any 24 words on his or her bingo card. Use the same directions you might use for regular bingo.

FOOTBALL BINGO WORDS

football	off sides	penalty	time out
touchdown	throw	grass	huddle
goal	scrimmage	field	punt
run	coach	goal post	defense
down	yards	kick	offense
quarterback	points	game	quarter
center	halfback	cheer	halftime
helmet	fullback	fans	score
spike	running back	cheerleader	team
tackle	uniform	bench	interception

FOOTBALL
BINGO
FREE
GO!
12

Football Player!

Make this cute football player from index paper. Add your favorite number to his jersey. Color, cut out and fold.

Stand several players on a tabletop and pretend to play your own championship game.

Students might like to make miniature football players to use as game markers for the game "Football Fever!"

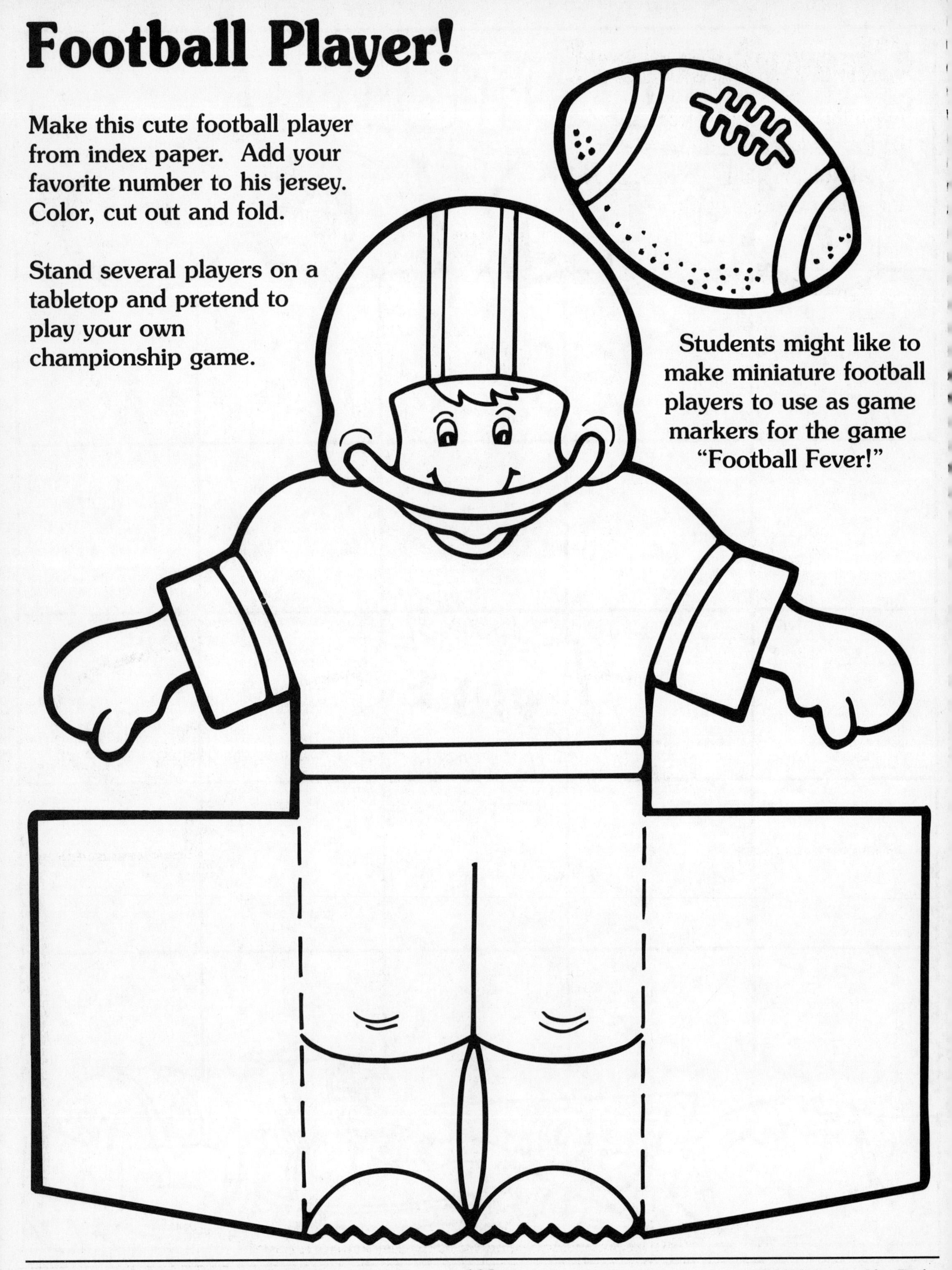

Cheerleader!

Make this cheerleader from index paper. Color, cut out and fold. Attach the pennant in one hand and the pompon in the other.

Football Fever!

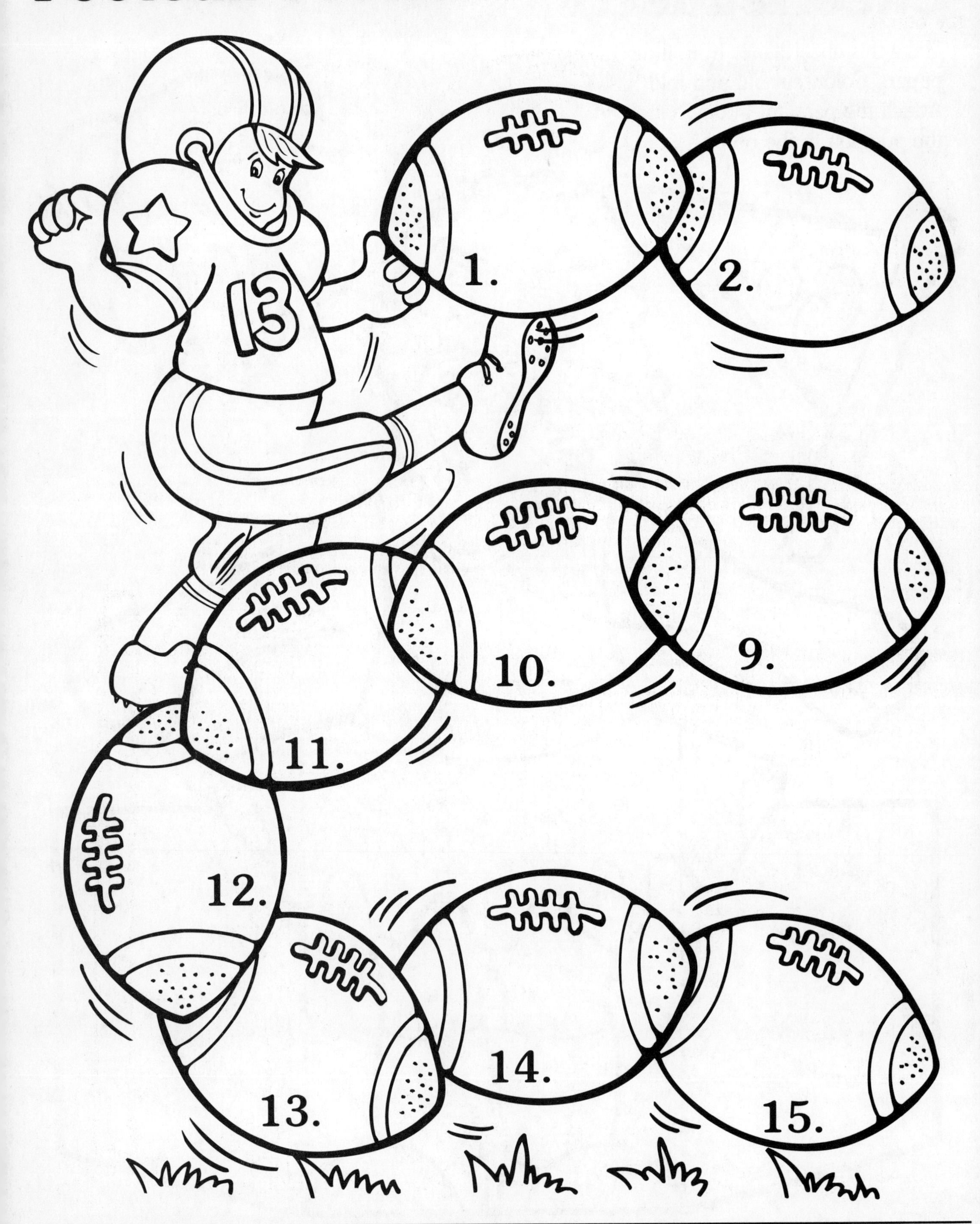

Teachers: Two, three or four children can play this game. Make your own task cards or write math problems on each football. Each problem must be solved before the player moves across the board.

Football Characters!

Enlarge these "Football Characters" for a fun and spirited bulletin board display.

Each student can make and label a football that can be passed across the board.

13

Creative Writing Footballs!

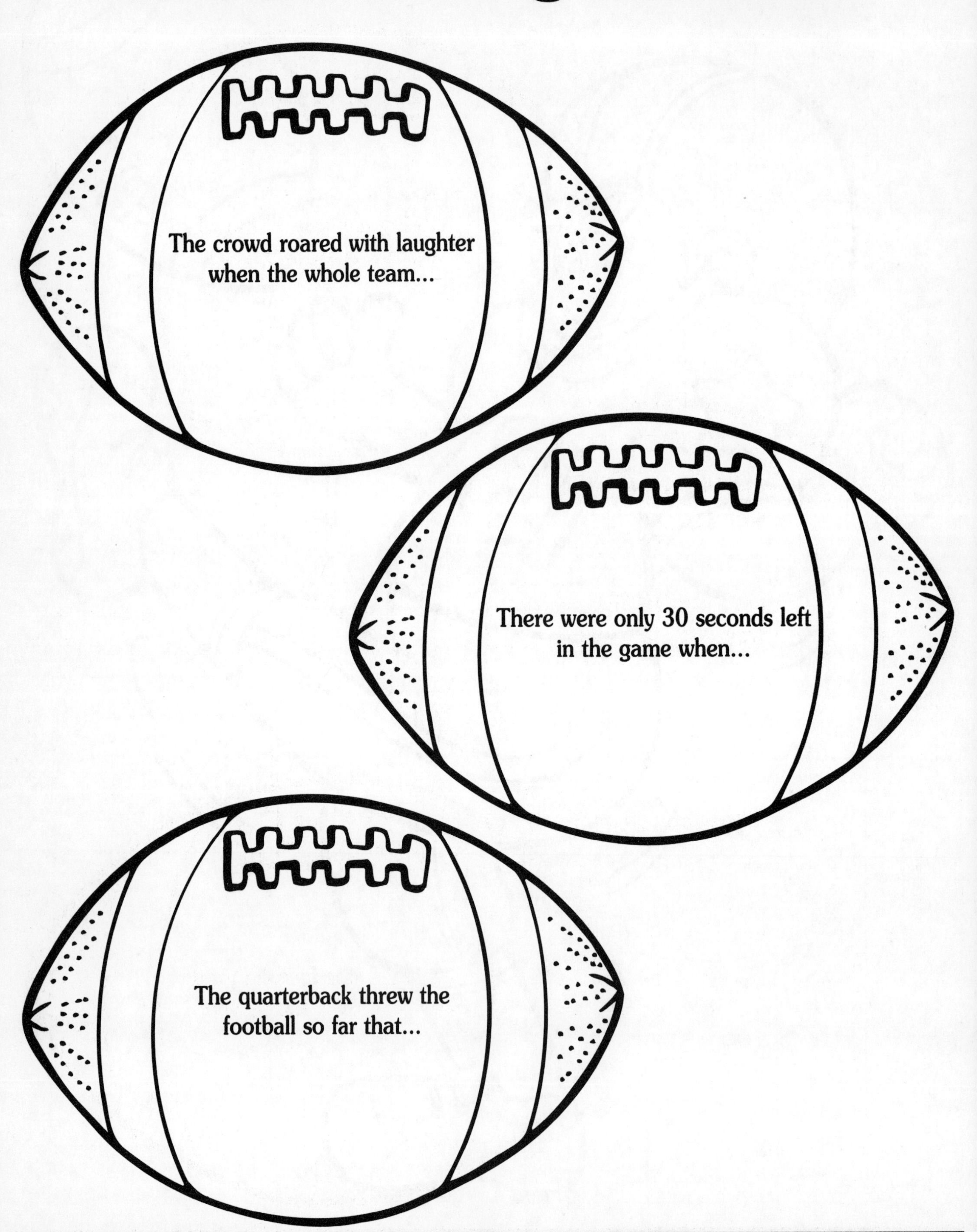

During halftime, the most amazing thing happened!

All of a sudden, the mascot from the other team...

Just then, the football went flying in the air and landed...

Football Booklet!

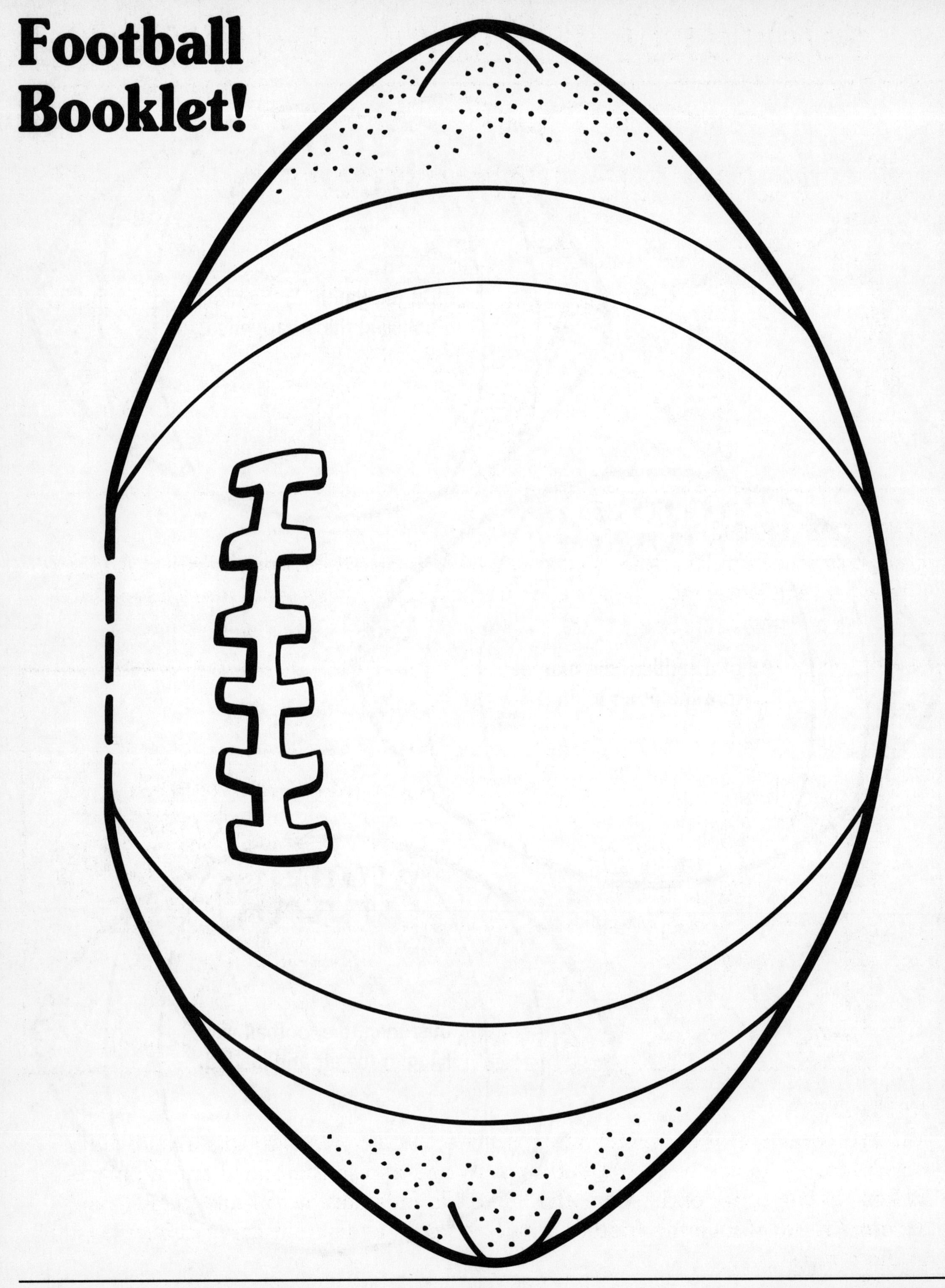

FOOTBALL BULLETIN BOARDS!

JOIN THE TEAM!
Hang colorful paper pennants across the class bulletin board. Write a student's name on each pennant. This is a wonderful way to welcome your students to the start of school!

KICK OFF!
Monitor your next PTA membership drive or fund raiser with this easy bulletin board idea. Display a set of goal posts at one end of the board and a "place-kicker" at the other end. Mark the "field" to indicate the various goals to be accomplished. Move the football down the field as your students collect points in the contest.

Design Your Team's Helmet!

Create a fictional football team and design their special helmet. You might like to write a story about your team or make up an original cheer. Perform your cheer along with several classmates.

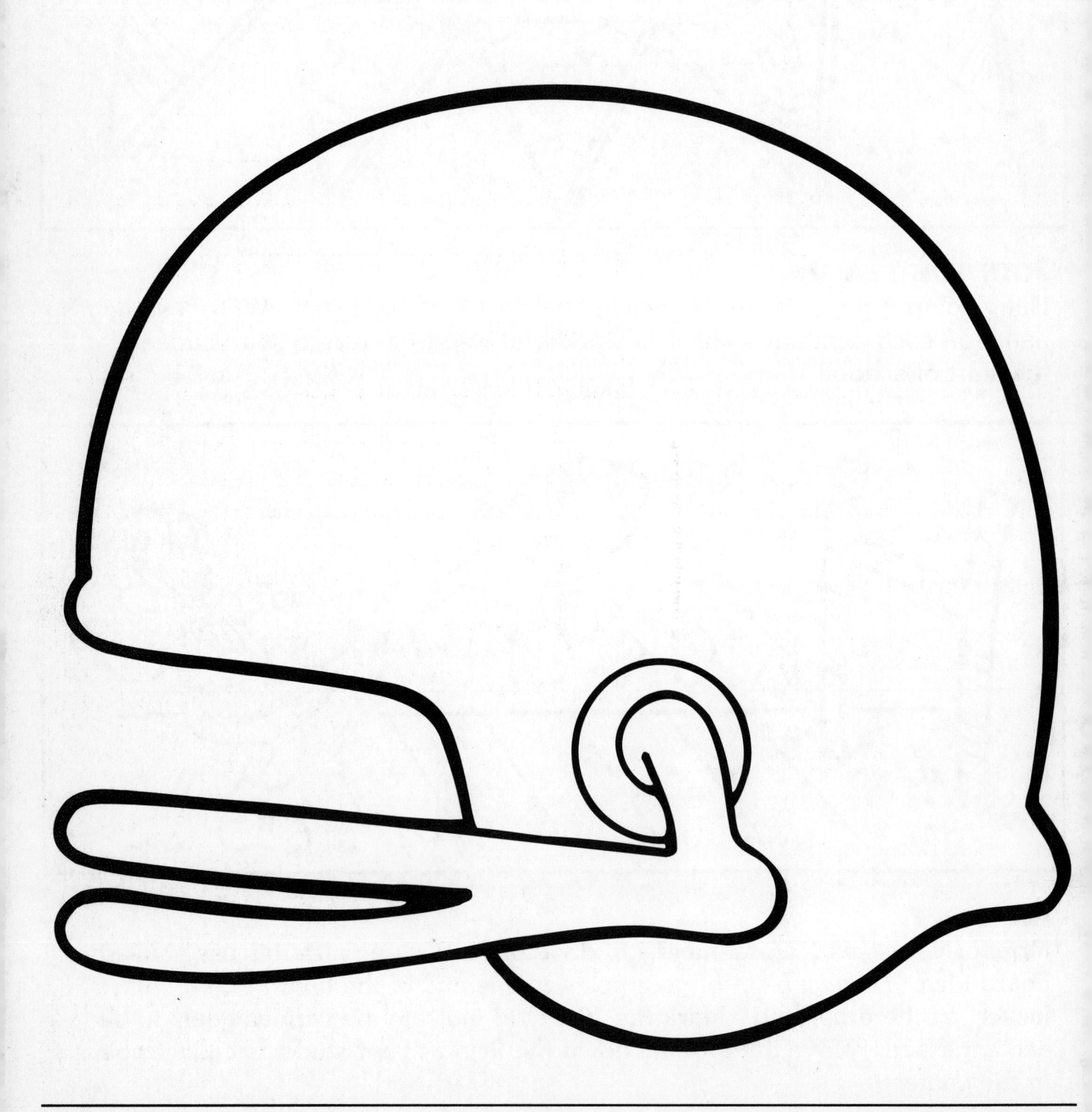